Radical Tenderness

A JOURNEY BACK TO ME —
HOW TO PAUSE, HEAL,
AND COME HOME TO YOURSELF

Lakeisha Gatling, PhD, LCSW, RYT

Copyright © 2025 Lakeisha Gatling, PhD, LCSW, RYT

Published and distributed in the United States by The Nourish Haven, LLC

ISBN: 979-8-218-88772-8

Cover design and interior formatting by Christy L. Staples of Get Launched!

Printed in the United States of America

All rights reserved. No part of this book may be used or reproduced by any means, graphic, electronic, or mechanical, including photocopying, recording, taping, or by any information storage retrieval system, without the written permission of the publisher except in the case of brief quotations embodied in critical articles and reviews.

This book is intended as a source of inspiration, reflection, and empowerment and should not be used to diagnose or treat any health condition. It offers insights drawn from personal experience, holistic practices, and personal perspective, but it is not a substitute for therapy, medical care, or other professional guidance. Every reader's journey is unique, and the practices described here may not be suitable for all individuals or circumstances.

The author encourages readers to honor their own needs and seek qualified professional support whenever necessary. Neither the author nor the publisher shall be held responsible for any outcomes resulting from the application of the ideas or practices shared in this book. This work reflects the author's lived experience. It is offered with compassion and care, but readers remain responsible for their own choices, actions, and well-being. The author and publisher disclaim any liability arising directly or indirectly from the use of this book. Any names used and details have been changed throughout this book to protect identities.

ACKNOWLEDGEMENTS

To God, thank you isn't enough. You have kept me close.

To my husband, thank you for holding my heart and creating a space for me to become tender.

To my mom, you are valued, you are important, and your story matters.

To my grandmother thank you for the assignment and the prayers which have been a driving force for my life's work.

To my family especially my sister-cousins, thank you for supporting and loving me through all my "weird ideas" LOL. Thank you for accepting who I have become.

To my dad and brother, I love and miss you.

To my Sister-Friends and The Nourishers, WE DID IT!! You have encouraged me along this journey of getting my words on paper. Your love, support and grace kept me focused especially during the times when I told myself, I shouldn't do this or that I couldn't do this. Thank you.

To the powerful authors, Alex Elle, Lalah Delia, Nedra Glover Tawwab, Clarindria Addison, you inspired me, encouraged me and helped me heal through your writing and teaching. I am forever grateful.

Lastly, to my community, thank you for sharing space with me.

CONTENTS

Author's Note   6

1: The Pressure to Pause: When Survival Mode Becomes Unsustainable   7

2: Choosing to Heal: A Sacred Invitation   10

3: The Tender Truth: When Pain Leads to Purpose   14

4: Honoring and Healing Your Younger Self: The Journey Beyond Hyper-Independence   23

5: Whisper No More: Claim the Power of Your Voice   35

6: Vulnerability: Embrace It   42

7: Codependency Is Not Love: Unhooking from Codependency   51

8: Hold Space for Your Grief: Making Room for Sorrow and Healing   61

9: The Radical Act of Self-Care: Reclaiming Wellness as a Necessity   74

10: I Thought Everything was Under Control: When Coping Strategies Begin to Fail   83

11: The Gift of Self-Compassion: Choosing Tenderness Over Tough Love   104

12: The Strong Friend: Releasing the Role and Reclaiming Your Needs   108

13: Faith Unbound: Losing Religion to Find Divine Love	117
14: The Arrival: Coming Home to My Body, Reconnecting Through Breath, Movement, and Presence	126
Epilogue	136
About The Author	138
Resources	139
Recommended Reading	140

Author's Note

This book is part story, part sanctuary.

It's a place where survival meets softness, where silence becomes voice, and where healing is not a destination—but a daily decision.
I wrote these pages for anyone who's ever felt like they had to hold it all together while falling apart inside. For the ones who've whispered their pain, masked their emotions, or carried more than their share. For the caregivers, the quiet ones, the strong ones, and the ones still learning to ask for help.

You'll find pieces of my story here—moments of panic, parentification, joy, grief, and growth. But more than that, you'll find invitations. To pause. To breathe. To reflect. To reclaim.

This is not a manual. It's a mirror. A soft landing. A reminder that your healing matters—and your voice deserves to be heard.

Take your time. Take what you need. Leave what you don't.

You are worthy of rest, reflection, tenderness, and radical self-compassion.

With tender loving kindness,
Lakeisha

1

The Pressure to Pause: When Survival Mode Becomes Unsustainable

I felt as if my world had come to a halt. It was becoming harder for me to sleep at night; my sleep was often filled with terror. The nightmares would not stop. I found myself feeling anxious, paralyzed with fear, and wondering, *how could I make it stop?* Until that point in my life, I had been able to make things stop. I could walk away or run away from things that hurt me. I could shut down when there was so much noise going on around me, but what I was feeling and what was happening in my body I could not control, and it scared the hell out of me.

At some point, I could no longer hide the reality from my husband that I was having nightmares. I would find myself waking up with uncontrollable tears, which began to wake him up too.

Many times, he held me to let me know that I was okay, even that felt foreign to me, because I hadn't experienced someone telling me that I was OK, that I was safe. It was from that moment that I knew something had to change, so I hit pause. Both my mind and body were urging me to pause and begin processing my experiences. That is how my healing journey began.

2

Choosing to Heal: A Sacred Invitation

Before you settle into the word healing, I would like you to consider what the word means to you. Grab a sticky note, piece of paper, journal, or even your phone to write out your definition. I invite you to define your own meaning because sometimes we allow concrete definitions to shape our beliefs or thoughts about wording.

Take a deep breath. I want to thank you. In this moment, you've given yourself permission to define your own meaning. That meaning will guide you along your path. Remember—your journey is yours alone, and it is uniquely beautiful.

Healing is a deliberate choice; It's an act of self-empowerment. The decision to heal empowers you to take control of your life in every way. Healing is a mind, body, spirit practice. Every action that you take along your journey will aid in personal growth.

Many of us have made the choice to heal due to experiencing a life event that has had a negative impact on our physical, psychological, spiritual, mental or emotional well-being. The event can be the starting point of the journey, but it doesn't have to be your only reason. My journey may have started due to trauma; however, trauma is no longer the reason that I stay on the journey. I continue to heal because I want to have healthy ways of dealing with life stressors, and I want to continue to grow and develop a healthy relationship with myself and others. I also continue because I am a human being who deserves to feel love, experience joy, and wholeness.

Why are you healing?

If you've listed names of people, such as extended family members or children, as the reason, I am thankful that you have chosen to change their lives in such an impactful way. However, I would like to encourage you to be your own reason. There will be days when you must think about others to gain the motivation to keep going, and that's ok. Keep in mind that this is your journey.

If you have not discovered your "why", here are some reasons to heal.
- To have a healthy connection with yourself and others.
- Emotional regulation.
- To address unhealthy behaviors.
- To ease emotional pain.
- To improve your outlook on life.
- The constant feeling that you do more for others than you do for yourself.
- You often feel overwhelmed.
- Because you want to experience a more fulfilled life.
- To deepen your faith and trust in the unfolding of your becoming.

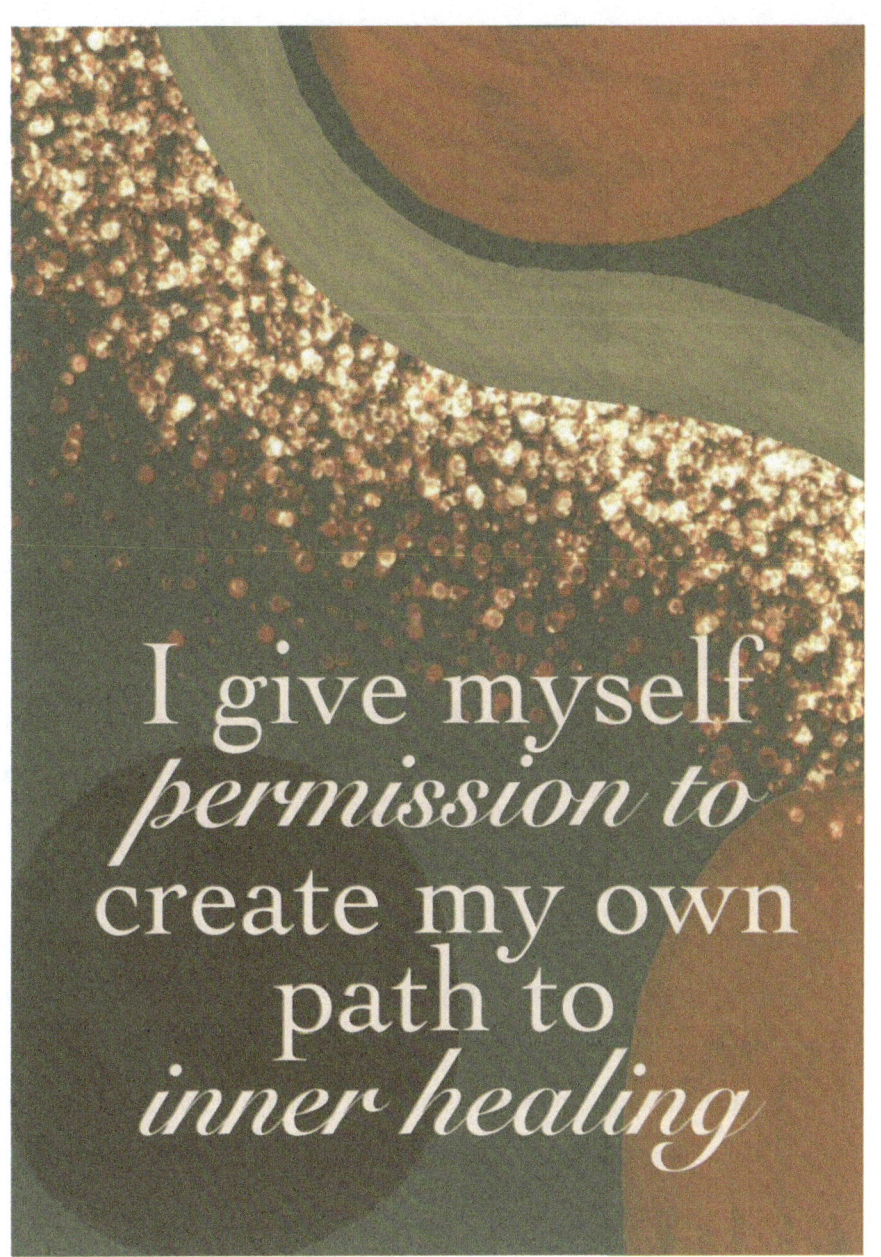

3

The Tender Truth: When Pain Leads to Purpose

When I was in my early 20s, I experienced what I considered to be a mental health crisis. I had my first panic attack; at the time, I had no idea of what a panic attack was or even what anxiety was. I just knew that I had this feeling of doom and worry that I could not get rid of. For some odd reason, I knew what I was feeling didn't feel like a medical problem. I didn't quite feel like I was going to have a heart attack, but more so felt like my world was caving in. I was having bad dreams, feeling restless, worried constantly, and having irrational fears that something bad was going to happen to me most days. Whatever this was, it wasn't going away. I did my best to act like I was okay.

Radical Tenderness

Deep down, I was having a tough time making sense of it all. I tried to go on as if nothing was happening. After all, I had been taught to "save face" and not to let people know my business.

For a couple of days after the panic attack, I carried on with life as usual. I continued to socially engage with family, friends, and my partner, who is now my husband. From the outside, everything looked normal, but that moment of normalcy was short-lived. I went to work one day, and my co-worker and close friend looked at me and said, "What is wrong?"

Apparently, as she described it, I looked like a deer caught in headlights. I could no longer mask what I had been experiencing and feeling. I explained what I was going through in the best way that I knew how, with tears streaming down my face, after listening, she said, "Keisha, you have to talk to someone". I agreed out of desperation and exhaustion from masking my experiences. Truth be told, I had symptoms of anxiety way before the panic attack happened.

During this time, we both worked at a major healthcare company; helping people find medical providers was a normal everyday task. She helped me find a psychologist who was close to my home so that I could begin the process of getting help in whatever capacity needed.

So, here I am, this 20-something-year-old young black woman, showing up in this posh Psychology office, not knowing where to begin.

With sweaty palms and scared out of my mind, my therapy journey began. I held the secret of my going to therapy for months before I told my family. Even that was contributing to my feelings of anxiousness because I felt as if I had failed, like I wasn't strong enough to keep it together.

It took some years for me to process all the things that contributed to my mental health decline. Through therapy, I learned how to name and express my emotions, reframe my thoughts, manage challenging family dynamics, and cope with my trauma history. I found my therapist to be extremely helpful; however, there were times during our sessions that I felt disconnected and a bit guarded, even though it was a proven safe space.

My therapist didn't look like me, and from the aesthetics of her office, it appeared that she had access to and the privilege of a lot more resources than I did. Towards the end of our time together, I felt better. I felt like there was a better version of me that evolved out of the therapeutic process. I thought about how much better my experience would be if I had been meeting with someone who looked

like me. I shared with my therapist that I wanted to help others, especially my community, in the way that she helped me. I will never forget hearing her say, "I believe you would be a great therapist."
I'm going to be honest, becoming a therapist was hard because I had to overcome the stigmas related to going to therapy, and now I was putting myself in the position to become one.

I knew there had to be others in my community who may have been suffering in silence like I was, and I wanted to help alleviate the suffering. So, I began the quest to become who I needed to see. A black therapist supporting my community and offering others the support that I had, but by someone who looks like us and can identify with our experiences.
If you are looking to begin or continue your healing journey, I would recommend starting by:
1. Giving yourself permission to start. Saying yes to your own needs is never a bad thing.
2. Acknowledge your emotions without criticizing yourself. Criticism could hinder your ability to address your needs.
3. Look for patterns that aren't going away. Those patterns are signals that call for your attention.
4. Don't wait until it feels too intense to begin your healing journey.
5. Don't be afraid to ask for help.

6. If needed, seek out support from a licensed qualified mental health professional.

As you sit with each chapter of this book, I invite you to **pause, breathe, and explore** —not to find perfect answers, but to deepen your connection with your own healing journey.

Radical Tenderness

Reflective Journaling:

- What does "healing" mean to you today? How has that definition evolved over time?
- What pain are you carrying that's asking to be witnessed, not silenced?
- What life experiences have nudged you toward healing? Which ones still echo in your body or spirit?
- Who or what do you often cite as your reason for healing? How can you center yourself in that narrative?
- What emotions do you tend to suppress or mask? What would it feel like to name them without judgment?
- When do you feel most overwhelmed or numb? What patterns or signals accompany those moments?
- What does emotional safety look like for you—and how can you cultivate it in your daily life?
- What fears or stigmas have made it hard for you to begin or continue healing?
- What does "giving yourself permission to start" look like when put into practice?

What does it mean to "become who you need to see"? Where and how are you already embodying the idea that you may have become who you need to see?

Lastly, who might you become if you allow yourself to heal?

Radical Tenderness

Radical Tenderness

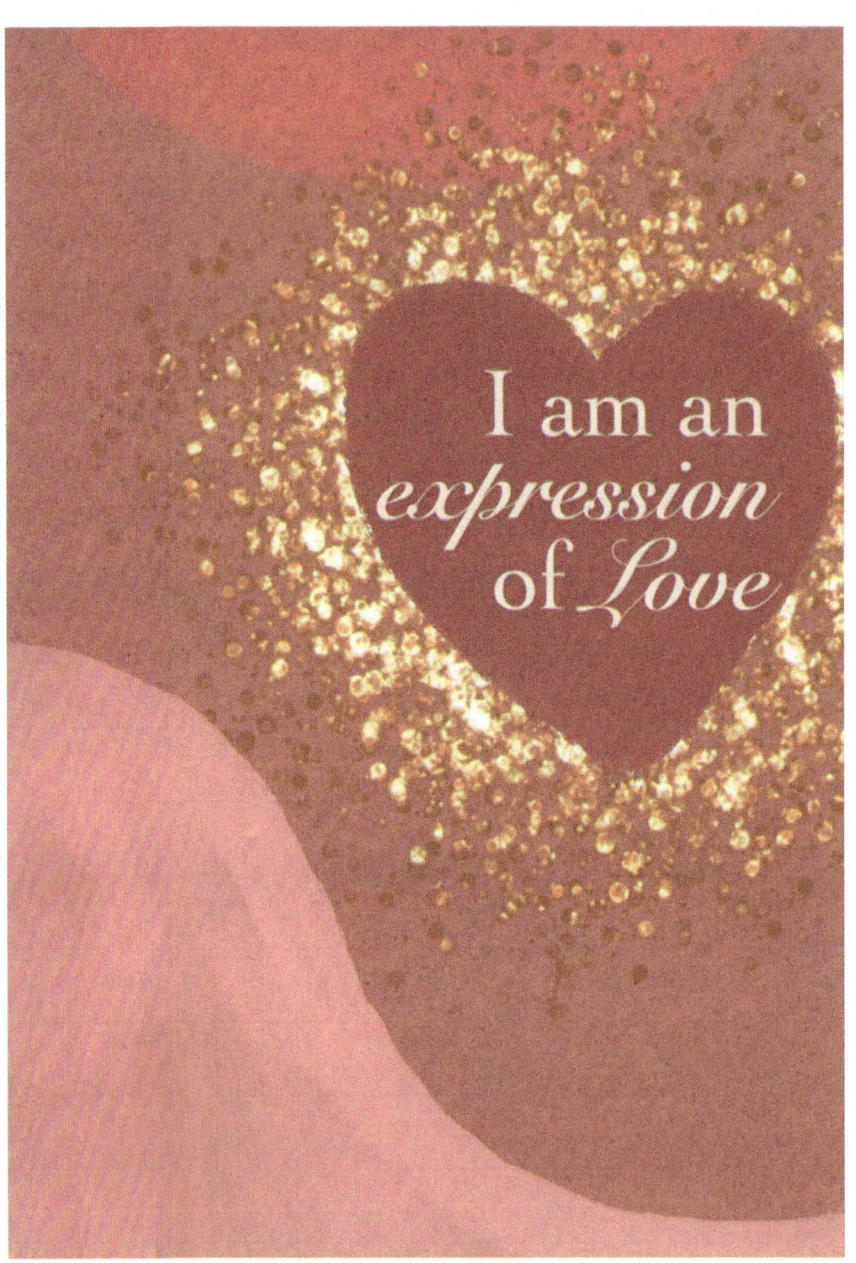

4

Honoring and Healing Your Younger Self: The Journey Beyond Hyper-Independence

I can remember as a little girl hearing my grandmother say to me. "I always prayed that you would take care of your mommy". In that moment, with my child-like understanding, I felt as though I had been given superpowers. I must've been between 7 and 10 years old at the time of the conversation. The popular comic He-Man and the Masters of the Universe was a cartoon that I often watched in my early childhood. She-Ra, the Princess of Power, was He-Man's twin sister. I loved her! I thought I was like her and had a magic sword of power and protection, which could help me take care of my mom. I understood. My responsibility was to protect my mom against any force that would try to come against her or us. I wasn't going to let anyone, or anything, hurt my mom. I can remember being so protective of her that I wouldn't even let her sleep alone, after all, I had a magic sword and not a fear in the world. I slept in bed with my mom until I was about 11. She had the hardest time getting me out of her bed. She tried extremely hard too. Sometimes she would lock her bedroom door, hoping that would prevent me from sleeping in her bed. She thought she tricked me one day and that the door locking would work, but I would sit in front of her door or sleep on the couch that was closest to her bedroom. I was determined not to let her out of my sight and wanted to ensure that she was always within my reach.

Can you imagine trying to get a child who is almost your size out of your bed? My mom is a very petite lady. She's 4'11" in stature, although, hear her tell it, she would say "I'm 5 foot even," which always gives me a little chuckle. My mom is the sweetest person I've ever had the pleasure of knowing. I mean, for real, for real, she is always so jovial. She will literally do anything for anyone. As a kid at our house, she was like the nursery rhyme, "The Old Lady who Lived in a Shoe"; she had so many children. She didn't know what to do (LOL). All the neighborhood kids would come to our house, and my mom would care for her nieces, nephews and extended family members' children during the summer while their parents worked. My mom was able to do this because she didn't work.

Radical Tenderness

She couldn't work, due to both her intellectual disability and the need to take care of my brother due to his medical needs and physical disability. My mom has struggled for most of her life with reading and writing and spent most of her school years in special education classes. This disability surely didn't make life an easy path for her. It was almost impossible to find a job. Despite her diagnosed disability and intellectual limitations, she did the best that she could to take care of us.

The other challenge that prevented her from working was the care that it took to meet my younger brother's daily needs. My brother and I are four years apart in age. My brother was born paralyzed. He spent the first 5 years of his life in a children's hospital, which was a two-hour drive away from our home. My mother and I would travel at least twice a month to visit him during his stay. The highlight of my visits with him were spending the night at the Ronald McDonald house because I knew I would get chocolate chip cookies. I can remember the smell like it was yesterday, the sweet aroma of cookie dough and chocolate as we entered the doorway to go to the front desk for our room assignment. The taste and warmth of the cookie always served as a source of comfort because what I was going to witness over the weekend was often a bit scary.

Radical Tenderness

There were children in the hospital of all ages with some incredibly challenging health issues. I can recognize my fear now as an adult, but I couldn't describe it in words as a kid, and seeing the children at the hospital eventually became my norm. I was such an inquisitive child, I would often find myself standing in doorways of hospital rooms, watching doctors and nurses care for patients. I remember going to a patient's doorway one day and watching the doctor as he was performing some sort of procedure, and he shut the door in my face. I ran down the hall and back to where I was supposed to be in the first place with my mom and brother. I guess that day, I was being a little too curious. I was so brave that the door didn't stop me from moving onto the next room, unbeknownst to me, more than likely this was the beginning of my childhood trauma.

After 5 years of traveling back and forth to the hospital, my mom was informed that my brother would be able to be discharged from the hospital permanently, but only with the help of 12-hour nursing care. Oh, happy day. This was a big deal. This was such a big deal that the local town news came to our home to interview my mom and brother for the news and the newspaper. I remember the day the newspaper journalist came, there were cameras and a whole crew. My brother was so happy, I can still see his smile now, bright and gleaming from ear to ear. All our lives changed from that moment forward.

My brother came to a new home, his own bedroom that he didn't have to share with a patient, he met extended family some whom he had never met before, and he was surrounded by an unfamiliar environment. My life significantly changed. I knew for sure I had a brother; I just didn't know he was supposed to live with me forever. I now have this new quest to conquer, which was to learn how to be a full-time sibling and how to take care of mom with our new family dynamic.

Daily, I watched from afar how my mom took care of my brother 24 hours a day, seven days a week. Although she had nursing staff to help her; she was pretty determined to learn and take care of him with a little assistance. She did just that, I watched her lift him in and out of bed, bath him, clothe him, feed him and take care of his medical needs. As I watched from afar gradually, I began to learn how to do things for myself. I started, combing my own hair, picking out my own clothes and creating my own world in my bedroom with my dolls and toys. My mom did not neglect to take care of me. In some way I thought I was helping by learning to do these things for myself and being strong by taking care of myself so my mom wouldn't have to. Little did I know this was my first encounter with parentification; I was a child taking on adult responsibilities. Some of the elders in my family and even extended family, would say things to my mom like *Wow, she combs her own hair. She's really a fast learner, or she is so smart.* Those words boosted my little ego, so I began to look for the next thing I could conquer on my own.

I wanted to learn how to cook. The first thing that I learned how to make was pancakes. I'll share a cooking secret with you that I learned. The best way to get an evenly cooked pancake is to wait until all the bubbles on the top half pop before flipping it over to cook on the opposite side. That will get you an evenly cooked pancake.

Before I knew it, I learned to wash dishes, separate, wash, fold clothes, and put them away. I thought the more things I learned, the less my mom would have to do or worry about me. While I could do all these adult-like things and chores, I was still very much a child and enjoyed doing child-like things. I would often retreat to my room. My room was fantasy land. I would create things such as doll houses. I would build my doll rooms out of plastic egg carrying crates, using folded cloths as furniture for the house and my mom's knick knacks as house décor. I also took my love for cooking back to my room. One day, I called myself, making donuts more like "do-nots". I rolled Play-Doh, made circles, and placed the rolled doh on top of the heating vent that was on my bedroom floor, so they could cook, since it wasn't real food. Over time as I continued with my experiments, pieces of Play-Doh fell into the heating vent. Guess who had trouble in her bedroom? ME. I tried to use a clothes hanger to get the donuts out and whatever else fell into the vent, without telling my mom. I knew I was going to get in trouble. It didn't work, so I had to tell her, I had to ask for help.

I thought I had to try everything on my own before asking for help. That survival-driven habit only reinforced my hyper-independence. Now, as an adult, I've learned to accept that it's okay to ask for help—even before I've run out of options. Please remember asking for help is not a sign of weakness. It's a reminder that you are worthy of support, care, and compassion.

Before we continue, I invite you to pause and honor your younger self.

There may be moments in my story that echo your own.
Take a moment.
Breathe.
Reflect on the tender beginnings of your journey — the ways your story first unfolded.

Set your Intention:
Soften the body, quiet the protector within, and offer compassion to the child who may have carried so much.

Breathwork Practice (5–7 minutes):

1. **Find Your Soft Space:**

Sit or lie down in a comfortable position. Let your hands rest gently on your belly or heart space.

2. **Inhale: "I was small, and I was strong."**

   Breathe in slowly through your nose for a count of 4.

   Feel your heart space and belly rise. Imagine the strength you held as a child.

3. **Exhale: "I don't have to be strong; I am safe to rest from being overly responsible."**

   Breathe out gently through your mouth for a count of 6.

   Let your shoulders drop. Let the cape fall.

4. **Repeat for 3-5 times.**

   With each breath, soften the parts of you that still feel like they have to be "strong."

   Let your breath be the tenderness that your younger self needed.

5. **Close with a Whispered Affirmation:**

   "I honor the child who carried so much." "I offer her rest, love, and light."

Radical Tenderness

Reflective Journaling:

- When did you first feel responsible for someone else's well-being, safety or happiness?
- What did protection mean to you then, and how has that meaning evolved?
- Can you recall moments that felt like play but were ways of coping or surviving?
- What did you learn about strength from your early childhood experiences?
- What did you quietly absorb by watching the adults around you?
- How did those observations shape your understanding of love, care for yourself and others?
- How did witnessing caregiving or your family dynamics shape your understanding of roles that you were supposed to take on?
- What messages did you receive about asking for help as a child?
- How do those messages show up in your life today?
- How do you navigate the tension between independence and vulnerability today?
- What role did imagination or creativity play in your emotional survival as a child?
- Are there ways you still create safe spaces for yourself through art, writing, or ritual? If not, what would you like to create?

Visualize the safe space, write down the details, create a plan to bring it to life.

Radical Tenderness

Radical Tenderness

5

Whisper No More: Claim the Power of Your Voice

Speak up, talk louder. Is there something the matter with your voice? Do you have a cold? Are you losing your voice? These were the questions that I would hear people ask and say as I was growing up, and I still get these reactions and questions today when people hear me speak. My voice has always had a unique sound and tone. I would like to say a unique sound applies to all human voices; no one voice sounds the same. My mom used to tell stories of how she would have to lay me on a pillow next to her when I was an infant, so she wouldn't miss hearing me cry, family members often told me stories of how they couldn't hear me, and that I had the softest voice they had ever heard. Of course, once I started school, kids begin to make fun of my voice and tease me.

Radical Tenderness

The sound of my voice and its uniqueness followed me around like a shadow. I was often described as the girl with the raspy voice.

When I was 12 years old, I joined a dance group. I love to dance. I contribute my love for dance to my older cousin. I have a host of cousins who are all similar in age. They were all my first friends; however, this cousin and I were the closest, more like sisters. She was a fashionista before we even knew that word existed. She was also the teacher when we played school, the cook when we needed a snack, and the dance teacher when we watched the latest music videos. Uh, oh, I'm aging myself (LOL). She would gather us up to learn a new dance routine on weekends, she was a little Debbie Allen. She had us learning every new dance move that you could think of, and we would have to perform it. Her passion for dance and teaching encouraged me to join the local traveling dance group and marching band in middle school.

Before you ask or wonder, I didn't play an instrument. I was a pom-pom girl in front of the band. Although I did have my run with the clarinet; I didn't play well enough to join any band. I was extremely excited about joining the dance group. We all had uniforms, which included T-shirts with our names on the back. Your name was given to you by the dance leader. I imagine it's much like a line name given in sororities. The leader named me "whisper".

Radical Tenderness

I thought *Oh, not again, another person mocking my voice*. But I wore the shirt anyway to every performance and adjusted to that being my team member name. Once again, I felt unseen and mostly unheard. A couple of years ago, my mother saw the dance leader at a local store while shopping, and of course, she asked my mom, *"How is Whisper doing? Does she still have that soft voice like a whisper?"* I'm sure my mom, as kind as she is, just smiled and told her all about how I had been doing. However, when the encounter was told to me, my nervous system was triggered, and all those childhood memories came flooding back within seconds.

My younger self had been whispering for quite some time. When will anyone hear me? The truth is, I had to begin to hear myself. I had to listen to my own voice. There were times in my life when I felt like I literally had no voice. My voice didn't matter, so I stopped talking. I stopped talking out of fear that I would encounter someone saying, "What's the matter with your voice?" and not getting past that point. As a result, I began to hesitate to speak in spaces and places where I felt I truly belonged. Still, the crippling fear led me to silence. I would only talk in small crowds or with family with whom I felt comfortable, but what I didn't know was that in my silence, I was still speaking.

My silence would soon be challenged.

College wasn't a subject that was discussed in my home. For many reasons, my mom's diagnosed intellectual disabilities, and my dad having been asked to leave school "put out" when he was in the seventh or eighth grade. According to my paternal grandmother, my dad had behavioral problems. He never returned to school. College was not the goal, and my parents had no experience with higher education to be able to support me through the process. My goal was to get a decent job and buy myself a Honda Accord. Work is what I know how to do. I got my first job at 14 and I haven't stopped working since then. I got my first corporate job in my early 20s and quickly learned that a degree would help me reach my goal of getting my Honda Accord, so I applied to a two-year trade school that also offered an associate of applied science degree program. I love school, I always have. I got great satisfaction out of writing, learning, and getting good grades. Also, I was working and paying for school. Getting low grades wasn't an option. I didn't have the flexibility or finances to take any class more than once.

Although I was mostly quiet amongst my peers at school, my grades began to speak for me. Some of the professors and instructors knew that I was working full-time and attending school full-time. Because of my academic performance and achievements, I was asked to be the valedictorian of my graduating class. I thought it meant to be like some kind of school mascot or maybe a class representative who sits in the front of the class at graduation. I immediately said yes with excitement. A couple of days went by, and graduation was approaching soon. I was asked by one of my professors, *"So, what are you going to speak on at graduation"*. My eyes must've popped out of my head like one of the cartoon characters when they are shocked internally. I said to myself, *"Oh shit, what did I agree to?"* I panicked and told my husband about the speech. He assured me I could deliver the speech. I ambivalently began the process of writing my speech. I solicited all kinds of advice. I wrote, revised, rehearsed, and panicked. I had to tell myself repeatedly, "You can do this. Just tell your story on graduation day." I did just that with my whisper of a voice, my palms sweating, my stomach having a dance party, and my throat feeling tight. I was reading from my handwritten paper in front of a crowd of at least 250 people, which included the school staff, graduates, and their extended family. I got near the end, and I looked up. To my amazement, I saw some with tears, some seeming awestruck, and others smiling with admiration.

I spoke up. My voice was no longer a whisper. I was a force. I was a storyteller. I was an encourager. In that moment, my voice seemed to matter, and it was heard. I learned that my voice had power and potential from that day forward, and my mission was to become more comfortable with speaking up and speaking out.

Radical Tenderness

Life sometimes has a way of silencing what should be heard, silencing what should be felt, and silencing what should be spoken. There's an unspoken rule in my community, which is that what goes on in my house stays in my house. What I've learned is that the house can be a literal house, or it can be the mind, body, and spirit of a human being. The saying means keep quiet; don't tell our family business (pain, secrets of troubles). For so long, my silence kept me in a place of discomfort, self-defeat, and fear.

Speaking brought ease to my soul. It made me feel that my existence mattered, and someone wanted to hear me.

When was the last time you allowed your voice to be heard?

When was the last time you honored your voice and told your truth?

Your voice is your power and deserves to be heard.

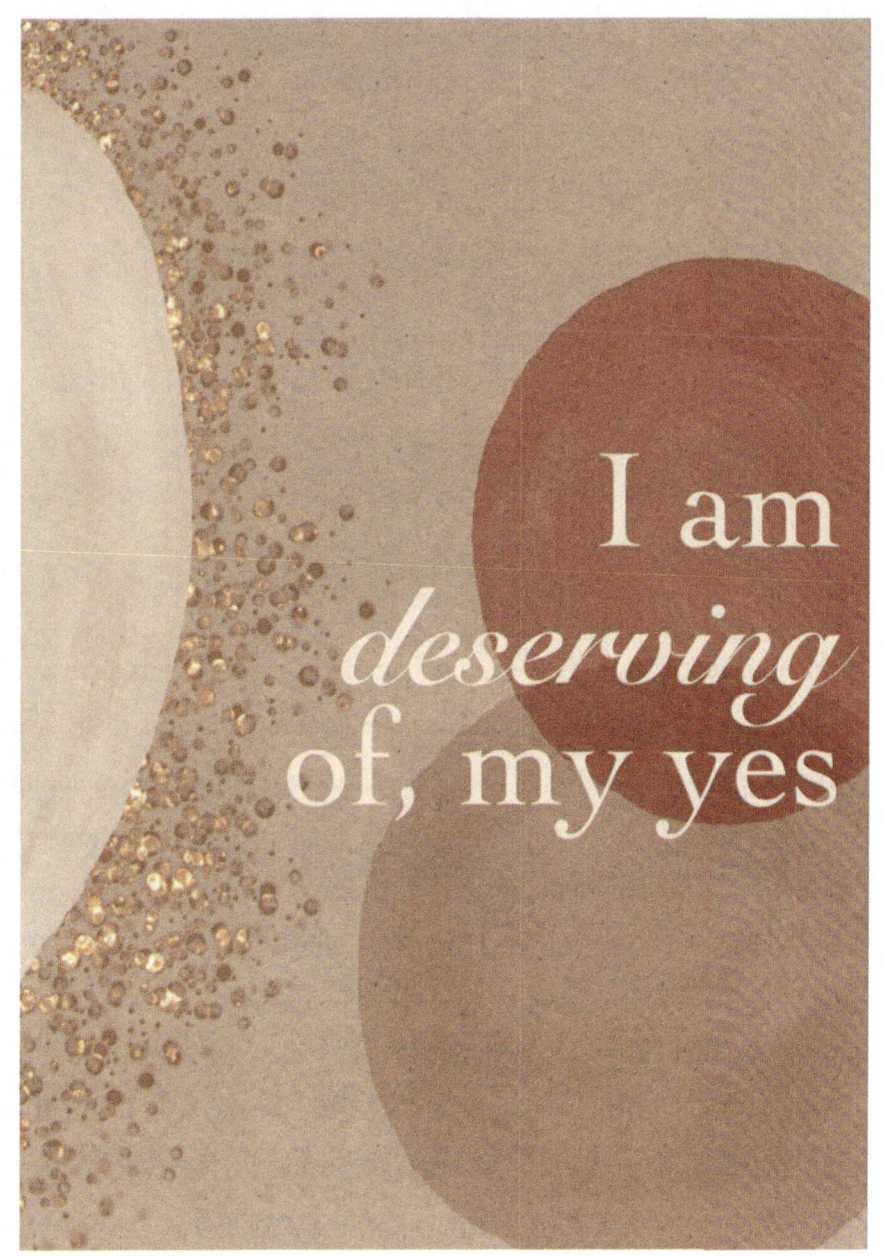

6

Vulnerability: Embrace It

Spaciousness has always been my comfort zone. If there is a crowded room, I would and I still do at times make it my business to sit away from the crowd. I often find a corner that will allow me to see the entire space of the room. In the corner, I can people-watch, observe behaviors, and bear witness to the emotions of others. Being away from the crowd has helped me feel comfortable and safe. The spaciousness was really a defense mechanism. What I was doing was avoiding interactions with people. I was distancing myself from the crowd based on the belief that if I could make myself small or unnoticed, no one could reject me. If I made myself "safe," then I wouldn't be judged. This avoidance showed up in every area of my life: school, work, and my relationships. In my formative years while at school, I would sit in the back of the classroom or as close to the door as possible. I knew that the students who sat in the back were less likely to be called upon by the teacher. When it came to college, every day for every class, I would arrive at class at least 10 minutes early and find a seat either in a corner or in the back row of desks. This way of being didn't work out too well while attending graduate school. Most of my classes were immersive learning experiences. One course in particular stays in my memory. This course was a counseling course; the focus of the class was to learn the art of therapeutic interventions. The professor put us in groups of 2, and we were instructed to role-play case vignettes. We had a scenario of a client, and one student was to take on the role of the client while the other was to take on the role of the therapist. The class was set up much like a fishbowl with two students in the middle "swimming" around trying to find their way. Everyone took their turns while the remainder of the students observed.

I knew it was getting closer to the time for me and my colleague to take our seats in the "fishbowl". My stomach began to do butterflies, my mouth became watery with a salt-like taste as if I were about to vomit, and my shoulders had this aching feeling of tension that I am 100% sure was visible to the class. The professor called my colleague's and my name; it was go time. We took our seats and got ready for the "session" to begin. We played out the case vignette while 20 or so Social Work students watched, took notes, and prepared to give us feedback. I could feel the heat rising within my body. I tried to play it as cool as I could by "masking" and getting into character. After all, masking was something I knew how to do very well. I had become a master at putting on a mask to appear as if everything was just fine.

The assignment turned into a real counseling session! I was feeling all my emotions as my colleague used therapy techniques to support me at that moment. We made it through the mock session, and to my surprise, many of the students shared thoughts on how well they thought we both did and how they were able to identify certain counseling techniques that we were all learning.

The masking was over.

After we completed our exercise, I remember feeling this huge feeling of release and returning to what I would consider to be my normal self. That day, I learned that there is healing in vulnerability. What I had been avoiding was a belief that I had and still struggle with at times today. I did not believe that it was okay to tell my truth or to share my experiences. I believed that silence equated to safety. I come from the culture of "what goes on in my house stays in my house." So, speaking in public about your problems, letting people see your emotions, or even hearing what you have to say about your feelings or family issues was a no, no. In that moment, while I was being put on "front street" (letting people see me and my vulnerabilities), I learned being vulnerable was a strength and not a weakness. It takes courage to share your story even if or when you do not feel ready. That day, in that class, sitting in the "bowl," allowed my courage to trump my fear. Instead of shrinking I leaned into my voice, my story, and the moment. I silenced a belief that no longer aligned with who I was becoming.

Never allow anyone or a situation to silence you. Your voice matters, and the first person that needs to hear you is YOU.

Pause to listen.

Set Your Intention:

Release the fear of being unheard and reconnect with the truth that your voice is sacred, powerful, and worthy.

Breathwork Practice (5–7 minutes):

1. **Settle In**

    Find a quiet space. Sit comfortably with your spine tall and your heart soft. Place one hand on your heart space and one on your belly.

2. **Inhale: "My voice is sacred."**

   Breathe in slowly through your nose for a count of 4.

   Feel the breath rise into your heart space. Imagine your voice filling your body with light.

3. **Exhale: "I speak with love and truth."**

   Release through your mouth for a count of 6.

   Let go of old stories that told you to stay quiet.

4. **Repeat for 5–7 rounds.**

   With each breath, soften the places that hold tension around speaking.

   Let your breath become your first language of truth.

5. **Close with a Whispered Affirmation:**

   "I am heard. I am whole. My voice is my superpower."

Reflective Journaling:

I invite you to reflect on your own voice— the whispers, the silences, and the power waiting to be spoken.
- When did silence feel safer than speaking?
- Were there moments when you chose quiet over visibility. What/who were you protecting? What were you longing for?
- What cultural or familial beliefs shaped your relationship with speaking out?
- Consider sayings like "what goes on in this house stays in this house." How did they shape your emotional landscape?
- How did you begin to reclaim your voice?
- What were the turning points for you? Was it through writing, storytelling, or advocating for yourself? How did you get the courage to speak up?
- What does your voice represent today?
- Is it a tool for healing, advocacy, connection, or truth-telling? How do you want to continue nurturing it?
- What does "masking" look like in your life today?
- What are you protecting, and what might you be ready to release?
- What parts of you still sit in the "corner", watching instead of participating?
- What would it take to expose the parts of you and how can you allow self-compassion to heal those areas?
- How has vulnerability helped you reclaim your voice?
- What truths are you ready to speak, even if your voice shakes?
- What does it mean to you to be brave in spaces that once felt unsafe?
- How can you honor your growth and your voice?

Radical Tenderness

Radical Tenderness

7

Codependency Is Not Love: Unhooking from Codependency

I thought if I did everything that my father asked me to do, he would love me and show up for me. Through my childlike eyes, I saw my dad as this gentle giant who would come to my rescue whenever I needed him to. My father was 6'2' tall, he had somewhat of a slender build, cocoa colored skin, and sandy brown hair. Most of my mother's family is short in stature, of course, my dad looked like a giant to me. I was a Daddy's girl. I always wanted to be with him. Being with him meant sleeping over at my grandmother's house. I never had to follow the rules. I got to eat mac and cheese with ketchup for dinner. Wear whatever clothes I wanted, even if I decided to wear the same outfit twice, and play with my cousins, his nieces and nephews, all day. Being with my dad was pure bliss, or so I thought. My dad and I would make blanket palettes on the living room floor of my grandmother's house, and that's where we would sleep for the night. Sometimes my dad didn't wake up until around noon, which would be just in time for us to watch the "stories". While he was sleeping, my grandmother would "fix" breakfast, which usually consisted of half a grapefruit with a teaspoon of sugar on it or cereal. After breakfast, we bathed, got dressed for the day, and then we would watch the news, 100,000 Pyramid, and The Price is Right.

To this day, I still have a love for game shows. Once the game shows were over, the midday news would come on again. My cousins and I knew what to do. We would gather whatever toys we were going to take outside to play with to the car porch because once the "stories" came on, there was no bothering my "Granny," as we affectionately called her. She was everything that you can imagine a "Granny" to be. She had the softest hands, soft skin, and she was plump (LOL). She wore house dresses most days of the week and sat in a rocking chair. All the grandchildren would attempt to sit on her lap all at once. Although she couldn't hold us all, she tried. She never really raised her voice at us, but we knew when we were in trouble. At any given time, you could find at least one of us hiding under her dress as she sat in her rocking chair. Hiding under her dress as she sat in her chair made us laugh so much; I can still hear our childlike laughter.

Radical Tenderness

My Granny was so loving that I never felt the absence of my father while I was at her house visiting for the weekends or whenever I wanted to be at her house. She welcomed everyone. Her love was so strong, it hid my father's addiction to alcohol and drugs. One of the reasons that my father made a pallet to sleep on the living room floor was because he was often too intoxicated to make it to his bedroom. His drinks of choice were Mad Dog 2020 and Thunderbird. When entering his bedroom, there were displays of empty bottles everywhere. His drug choice was crack cocaine.

On Friday nights after working odd jobs, he would walk to my mother's house, which was about 3 miles from my Granny's house, and pick me up to stay with him for the weekend. He would walk the 3 miles with me either on his shoulders or holding my hand all the way back to my Granny's house. While on those walks, he always made promises to take me shopping for toys or clothes. Because he worked odd jobs, he received his paychecks in cash. Once we arrived at my Granny's house, Dad would fix something for me to eat and then hand me his cash. He told me to hold onto it so that we could go shopping the next day. Knowing that I was going shopping for toys and clothes always made me excited. What kid doesn't want to shop for toys! I held onto the cash and the idea of going shopping the next day. The next day never came. My father was dropping me off with my Granny and would leave and come back and forth to the house throughout the night to ask me for his money. It was my responsibility to give him the money.

Eventually, the money was gone, and so was the dream of shopping. This pattern continued for quite some time. I was too young to realize that my father was struggling with addiction, and I had become codependent on his addictive behavior. I was enabling his behavior without knowing it. My father relied on me to ration out his paycheck, and I relied on the promises that he made me. I thought that if I continued to do what he asked, I would eventually receive the promise. Our love felt more like a barter system; I was trading him money with hopes of receiving his love, his presence, and his promises. Our relationship continued with the same pattern up until he died. My father struggled deeply, which led to him being in and out of jail, broken relationships with family, sickness, and homelessness.

I tried my best to care for my father, which included me becoming the Power of attorney over his social security disability and medical decisions. I tried to do for my father what he couldn't do for me. I hoped that my love would cure his addiction, and it did not. He was never able to be a father to me, but I mothered him to the best of my ability. Hoping that one day he could be the father that I looked up to. My healing journey and work in therapy have allowed me to come to terms with our relationship, what it was and what it was not.

Radical Tenderness

I am grateful for all the things that our relationship taught me and the role that it played in my healing journey. I learned how to give up being overly responsible for people.

The first person that you must be responsible for is YOU.

I learned to make space for my own feelings and unmet needs.
Your needs matter too, and most importantly, love does not "fix people". You cannot and should not trade your love to be seen, heard, or valued.

Pause to "Unhook from Codependency"
This breathwork sequence is for those moments when your body still remembers the weight of waiting, the ache of over giving, and the hope that love could fix what it couldn't.

Set Your Intention:
Find a quiet space. Sit or lie down. Place one hand over your heart, the other over your belly. Let your body know it's safe to rest.

Breathwork Practice (5–7 minutes):

1. **Grounding Breath**

    Inhale through your nose for 4 counts

    Hold for 2 counts

Exhale through your mouth for 6 counts.

Let your shoulders drop. Let your jaw soften.

2. **Release Breath**

With each exhale, silently say:

"I release what's not mine to carry."

Imagine old agreements, expectations, and roles gently loosening their grip.

3. **Self-Compassion Breath**

Inhale: *"I am worthy of love."*

Exhale: *"I honor my own needs."*

4. **Closing Integration**

Return to natural breath.

Imagine a soft light filling your heart space.

Whisper to yourself: *"Love is not earned. I am already enough. I am LOVE."*

Radical Tenderness

Reflective Journaling:

For the Tender Work of Letting Go

These prompts are meant to meet you where you are—softly, honestly, and with room to breathe:

- What did you learn about love growing up?
- What parts of that story still live in you, and which parts are you ready to rewrite?
- When have you felt responsible for someone else's healing?
- What did that cost you emotionally, spiritually, financially or physically?
- What promises did you hold onto that were never fulfilled?
- How did those promises shape your sense of worth or belonging?
- What does it look like to mother yourself in the ways you may have mothered others?
- What do you need to feel safe, seen, and supported now?
- What does love feel like when it's not transactional?
- How can you practice non transactional love with yourself?

Radical Tenderness

Radical Tenderness

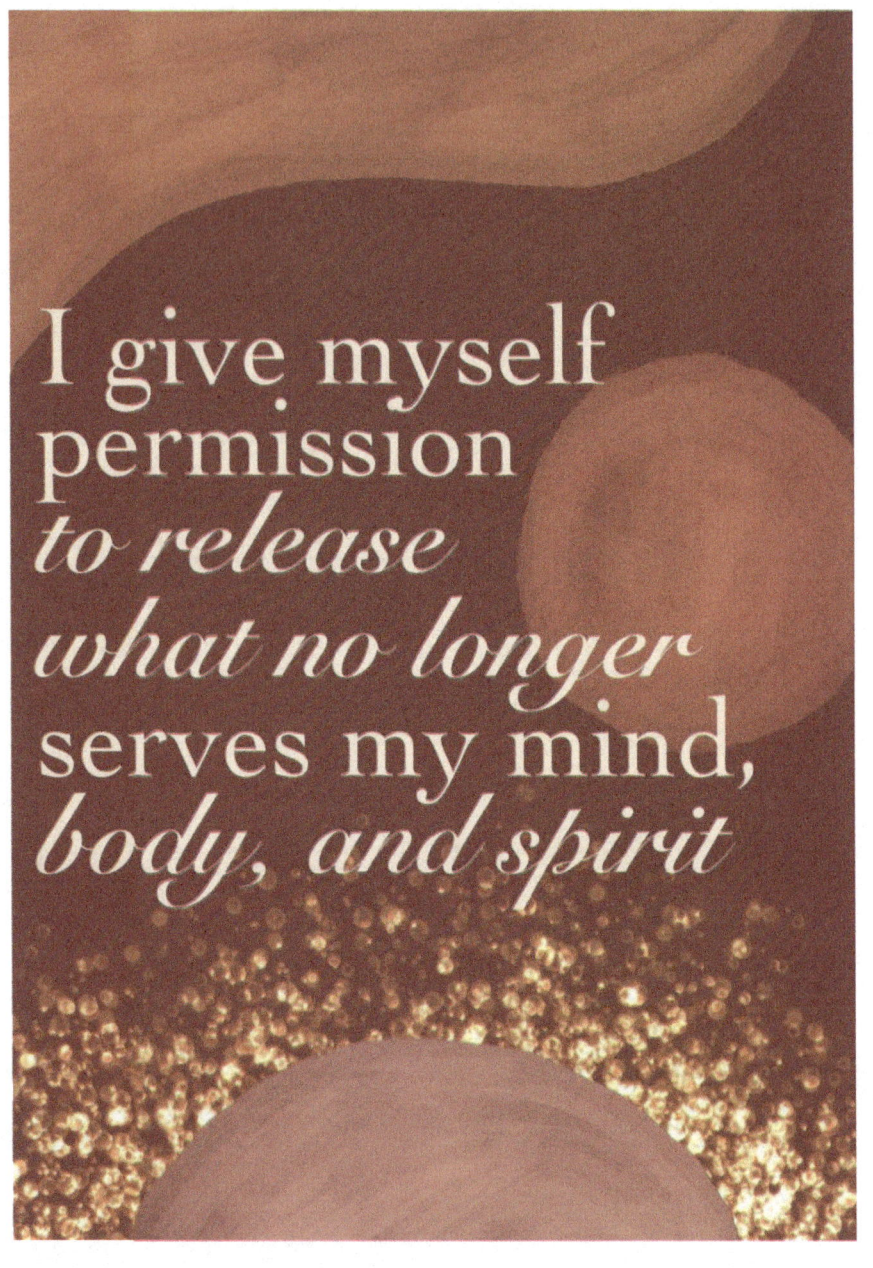

8

Hold Space for Your Grief: Making Room for Sorrow and Healing

Grief is a word that we are all too familiar with, and it's an experience that happens more than most of us care to acknowledge. Towards the end of my undergraduate degree program, I volunteered to assist with an 8-week support group that was held at a local church. During the first meeting, I heard stories about the loss of loved ones, divorce, job loss, and health loss due to illness.

After the group shared their stories and why they decided to attend, the group facilitator made a statement that has stuck with me for years. She looked at the group with an empathetic expression and a calm voice, and said, *"Grief is God sized."* At that moment, I don't think I really understood what she meant, and to be honest, I wasn't confident enough to ask. In retrospect, what I believe she meant was there is no true formula for healing through grief, and often the emotions associated with grief are more intense than we can handle at times.

I wanted to learn more and continued to help. I completed my volunteer work and learned how to support those who are grieving from a Biblical point of view and how to be supportive in a structured way. Unbeknownst to me, I would need those words that the group facilitator offered in the near future. Several months after my volunteer work, I completed my undergraduate degree and prepared myself for the next chapter of my education, which was graduate school. Graduate school was required for me to do the work that I envisioned myself doing, which was to become a social worker, help people, and educate myself enough so that I could care for my brother should I need to take on the caregiver role if my mother was no longer able to, whether it be due to a decline in health or death.

As a trauma survivor, I have spent a great amount of time and energy preparing for the "what if". Becoming a social worker also became a part of the "what if" plan. Growing up with a sibling with disabilities meant that there were constant caregivers in our home. A social worker would visit us every month, and it was her job to become familiar with the family and ensure that my brother was receiving the care he needed. Whenever she arrived, she got out of her car with her briefcase and sat at our kitchen table with her notepad, documenting her interview with my mom and my brother's nurses. Even then, I knew her job was important, and she seemed to be the one to keep everything together. While my primary goal was to practice therapy, I also figured that my degree would help me take care of my brother. I did all the things that I needed to do to get into graduate school, which included test preparation for the GRE, getting letters of recommendation, reviewing our finances because the program required full-time attendance, and restructuring my life to work part-time and attend graduate school. The program recommended not working at all to allow for the focus to be completely on our studies. I couldn't imagine not working at all as an option for me. I found a job that allowed me to work 25 hours a week, which was just enough to pay my share of the bills. The struggle was real! In fact, the reason that I had to look for another job was because of the full-time job that I had at the time retracted their initial agreement which was for me to transition to part-time once my program started.

Two weeks before school started, I was called into the office by my manager and informed that the company needed me full-time and would not be able to accommodate my request for a decrease in hours. My first reaction was fear; it was the fear that I wasn't going to be able to attend the program that I had worked so hard to get into. I called my husband as soon as I was notified.

I was so distraught that I could barely work for the rest of the day. I went into the bathroom while on my break and cried. That night, my husband and I talked about the pros and cons of me not working at all and what that would mean for our household. It would have been really tight financially, but we could have made it work. He told me to quit, and that's what I did the next day. I walked into my manager's office that morning with an elevated heart rate, sweaty palms, butterflies in my stomach, and handed in my resignation.

The idea of quitting my job without having one lined up was a huge trigger for me. I have worked since I was fourteen years old, and although my husband is a great provider for us, the idea of me being dependent on him scared the hell out of me. I felt like I was losing my ability to take care of my needs. I had to trust that it was all going to work out. It wasn't easy, but it worked out.

Grad school started, and I had begun to feel comfortable with this new, temporary way of living, which included being in a classroom with adults who were both younger and older than me and being on a college campus as opposed to an office during the day. I attended classes both during the day and in the evenings. I was becoming acquainted with this new season of life and a new way of experiencing college. I was enjoying the new people that I met in my cohort and worked diligently to stay abreast of all my coursework.

Radical Tenderness

Even though things had been challenging to start, for once, I started to believe and feel that things were going smoothly and working out just as I had planned. Unfortunately, that feeling and belief came to an abrupt stop. During the fall of my first full year of graduate school, my life changed forever. My husband and I were out shopping for a new car, and while he was talking with the sales associate, I excused myself to go use the restroom. Upon returning from the restroom, there was an eerie feeling in the place. My husband walked towards me, and he had an expression on his face that I had never seen before. He placed one hand on my shoulder and said, *"We need to go."*

I looked at the sales associates with a smile on my face and said, *"What did you do to my husband while I was away?"* The sales associate did not return the smile or joking tone. He looked at me with a very stoic facial expression. I was really confused at that point. We reached the car, and my husband asked me to call my grandmother because she had been trying to reach me. In that moment, I knew something was wrong; I could feel it all over, especially in the pit of my stomach. The words I heard I will never forget: *"Your brother died"*.

She couldn't be talking about my brother, the one I had just spoken to the night before. The only sibling that I had, the one with whom I could laugh and joke with about our crazy childhood. The one who had beaten all the odds. The one who thought I was the best sister on this God-given earth. The one who never called me by my name and only addressed me as "sister". That's exactly who she was talking about.

From that day forward, it has felt like a part of me is missing. The pain was so unbearable that I pushed it aside so that I could complete my degree. I thought that this was another moment for me to show that I could be strong. Being strong meant holding it together and holding onto myths that didn't really help me with my pain. There came a point when I could no longer hold onto the idea and behavior of "being strong". Grief took over. This was one emotion that I could no longer push away. It was showing up when I least expected it whether it be watching a movie, seeing siblings together, or even hearing someone talk about their own siblings. I had to do my own inner work and allow space for grief to move through me.

Grief has a way of becoming a teacher. Grief taught me to how to sit with pain without a timeline. There is not a "correct" way to grieve. Grief responds to the relationship itself, not the title or role that the person played in your life. You don't have to "get over" anything. You can work through your pain when you feel ready and not a moment sooner. Grief also holds duality; joy and pain can coexist.

Your healing through grief will require self-compassion and gentle patience with yourself.

Pause to hold space for your grief.
Make space for what often feels unbearable. Find a quiet space, gather items for comfort (tissue, tea, blanket, journal, pen). Give yourself permission to make space to work through what often feels unbearable. Allow yourself to grieve.

Breathwork Practice (5–7 minutes):

Set Your Intention:

Create space for grief without needing to fix or rush it. This practice invites the body to soften around what feels too big to hold alone.

Posture: Seated or lying down, supported by cushions or a blanket. Eyes closed or gently softened.

1. **Grounding Breath**

    Begin by noticing where your body meets the earth.

    Feel the weight of your hips, your back, your feet.

    Whisper to yourself: *"I am here. I am held."*

    Let your breath move naturally for a few cycles.

2. **Wave Breathing**

   Inhale slowly through your nose for a count of **4**

   Hold gently for **2**

   Exhale through your mouth for a count of **6**

   Pause for **2** before the next inhale.

   Repeat this cycle for several minutes, imagining each breath as a wave washing over you.

   On each exhale, silently say: *"I release what I cannot carry."*

3. **Heart-Center Expansion**

   Place one hand over your heart, the other on your belly.

   Inhale: *"I welcome what is."*

   Exhale: *"I soften around my sorrow."*

   Visualize your heart space expanding—not to erase grief, but to make room for it.

   If tears come, let them. If numbness arises, honor that too.

4. **Integration + Stillness**

   Return to a natural breath.

   Let your body rest in the stillness.

Radical Tenderness

Whisper: *"Grief is not a problem to solve. It is a presence to honor."*

When you're ready, gently open your eyes or place your hands in prayer at your heart.

Reflective Journaling

Before you begin writing, I want to remind you: there is no right way to grieve, and there is no timeline for your healing. These questions are not meant to fix or rush you. They are here to hold space—for your sorrow, your memories, your resistance, and your resilience.

You are invited to show up just as you are.

With your full heart or your numbness.

With your clarity or your confusion.

With your tears, your silence, or your laughter that surprises you in the middle of the ache.

Let this be a space where you don't have to be strong.

Let this be a space where you can be honest.

Let this be a space where your grief is not too much.

Take a breath.

Place your hand over your heart.

And when you're ready, begin.

Radical Tenderness

- How has this grief changed you—and what parts of you are still intact?
- What do you need to forgive yourself for in this process?
- What rituals or practices help you feel connected to what/who you've lost?
- What does healing look like for you—not as "moving on," but as moving through?
- What kind of support feels nourishing right now?
- What did grief teach you that no one else could?
- Where have you mistaken survival for healing?
- What myths about strength are you ready to release?
- How do you honor the relationship, not just the role, of those you have lost?
- What does self-compassion feel like at this moment?
- What would it mean to give yourself permission to feel joy again after loss?

Radical Tenderness

Radical Tenderness

9

The Radical Act of Self-Care: Reclaiming Wellness as a Necessity

When I started drafting this book, I had every intention of making it fluffy and sound easy. But that is not my reality. My life has not been fluffy, nor has it been full of ease. Self-care is no different. Self-care was very much something that I viewed as a privilege. I thought self-care consisted of having spa days and hair and nail appointments. I viewed it as something I couldn't access because of my socioeconomic status, and it was not a concept I was taught. Also, when I saw pictures of women relaxing, most of the pictures did not look like me, which further played into my belief that self-care was for the privileged.

I understood self-care in its basic form: keep your body clean and make sure you "look presentable". Self-care is much more than relaxing, and just like my life has not been fluffy or easy, neither is your self-care journey. The journey of self-care can feel like Elizabeth Kubler Ross' stages of grief: anger, denial, bargaining, depression, and acceptance. Initially, when I learned about self-care, I was angry that I had not become aware sooner. I denied that it needed to become a part of my life. I bargained with myself repeatedly about why it was important, even if no one else agreed with what I was doing. I felt depressed at times because the journey felt lonely and isolating; I was introducing a new concept into my life that no one I knew was talking about or practicing. Most importantly, I had to come to a place of acceptance that it was something that I needed to do for me, no matter what.

My family's culture is to help and take care of others. Literally, most of us are in the helping profession in some way. Both of my maternal grandparents worked and retired from being caregivers in both the medical and mental health fields. I grew up watching my mom care for my brother; therefore, helping and taking care of others was the cultural norm for me. Putting the needs of others first was also normal. I witnessed countless times of my mother putting her needs last, even if it was serving herself last at dinner. Experiencing the role of caregiving in the way in which I did taught me that others come first.

Radical Tenderness

The belief that the needs of others must come first was challenged during my first semester of graduate school in my Master of Social Work program. I can remember the excitement and eagerness to start the program because I felt like I finally made it! I was closer to my goal of becoming a therapist, and it was a very long road to get there. Being a working adult and full-time student simultaneously is no easy feat. I have a great deal of respect for anyone who works while attending school, raising a family, and serving in the role of a caregiver.

Honestly, by the time I started graduate school, I was already experiencing symptoms of burnout. I was often overwhelmed, emotionally, and physically exhausted. My life had been full of responsibility from an early age. I had no understanding of what burnout or compassion fatigue even was. When I received my schedule for my core classes and saw that there was a required course titled "Self-Care", I was curious and a little confused. I thought to myself, *"What does self-care have to do with social work?"* I quickly learned. Self-care has everything to do with the social work profession. It is included in our ethical guidelines, and we are humans supporting humans, of course we should take care of ourselves. The efficacy of our work is not just based on theory and technique. How we show up to support our clients begins with self-awareness and self-care.

Self-care begins with self-awareness because we cannot tend to what we do not recognize. As part of cultivating self-awareness, we completed a self-care assessment to recognize the practices we wished to sustain, let go of practices that no longer served us, and discover new opportunities for growth. The assessment provided clarity, which then allowed us to move to the next step, which was to create a self-care plan that was sustainable. This assignment was not easy at all. It caused a purposeful pause. Each question on the assessment required self-inquiry. It challenged every area of self-care: physical, emotional, spiritual, financial, and relationships. After completing my assessment, I realized that I had little to no practice at all. How could I have practiced? I had not considered my own needs. I was focused on surviving and being able to provide for myself and my family financially. I believed that I had to be responsible for everyone in my immediate family (Mother, Father, and Brother), which caused me to neglect myself.

The class was everything that I did not know I needed for my own healing journey. My self-care began with the radical act of saying to myself, *"I matter, and if I keep living with the weight of the world on my shoulders, I will continue to suffer. I have the power to alleviate my own suffering."*

Radical Tenderness

Therefore, I started implementing what I consider to be a form of radical self-care. I began resting from people, places, and things that were not truly serving me. I also set much needed boundaries with myself. I had to unlearn the behaviors and habits that I had which contributed to my overwhelm and exhaustion.

Radical self-care is a deliberate choice. It is the practice of tending to your emotional, physical, and spiritual needs with urgency and reverence. Radical self-care is not an isolated decision when something traumatic happens. It is a deliberate choice to continuously choose yourself, even when it feels hard.

"Caring for myself is not self-indulgence, it is self-preservation...."
--Audre Lorde

You have the power to alleviate your own suffering.

How could the concept of radical self-care change your life?

Reflective Journaling

I invite you to create a self-care plan by using the journal prompts as a guide. Consider all aspects of your being: Emotional, Psychological, Physical, Spiritual, and Relationships.

Reclaim Your Mental Space

- What thoughts or beliefs have you inherited that no longer serve your well-being?
- Where do you feel most mentally free—and how can you create more of that space?
- What does it look like to say "no" without guilt?

Honor Your Emotional Truths

- What emotions have you been suppressing to keep others comfortable?
- What does emotional safety feel like in your body?
- How do you want to be supported when you're not okay?

Nourish the Body with Intention

- What does your body need today—not to perform, but to feel loved?
- How do you want to move, rest, or nourish yourself this week?
- What practices help you reconnect with your breath and your body?

Radical Tenderness

Set Boundaries as Liberation

- Where have you been overextending—and what's the cost?
- What boundary would feel revolutionary to uphold?
- How can you lovingly remind yourself that you are your first responsibility?

Center Joy

- What brings you joy that you've been denying yourself of?
- How can you make space for pleasure without apology?

Reimagine Self-Compassion

- What does radical self-compassion sound like in your inner dialogue?
- What would it mean to treat yourself like someone you deeply love and respect?
- How can you celebrate yourself today—not for what you've done, but for who you are?

Radical Tenderness

Radical Tenderness

10

I Thought Everything was Under Control: When Coping Strategies Begin to Fail

I found myself having sleep disturbances again. I continuously passed it off and thought, *"Oh, this is just stress; it will go away after this week is over."* During that time, I had several stressors in my life. I felt as though the business that I worked hard for was failing. The money coming in wasn't as consistent as it had been in the past, and the phone wasn't ringing with new clients seeking services. I tried to convince myself that this was just a part of the "job" as a solopreneur. Every business has its ups and downs, and maybe this is just a season of low volume. I was carrying the weight of the business on my shoulders.

Radical Tenderness

I wear many titles which include CEO, CFO, Admin, bookkeeper, policy maker, policy enforcer, payroll, appointment scheduler, and therapist. Sounds like a lot, huh? It can be, and graduate school doesn't teach therapists how to start and manage a private practice. Many of us clinicians are opening practices and learning as we go. This situation is not unique to therapists; I am sure most first-time business owners with no blueprints are learning as they go. At the time of this sleep issue, I had been in business for 6 years. Surely, I should have figured it out by now, and everything should be running smoothly. I tried to do everything that I could to create a sustainable business. I sought professional support from other therapists who had been practicing for years before me. I attended courses that taught how to run a successful practice and consulted with other types of business owners to gain insight into areas such as business marketing and financial structure. It felt as though nothing was working.

The truth of the matter is that the practice wasn't running smoothly because I wasn't doing well mentally. I was stressed, overwhelmed and dealing with a lot of uncertainty. Although my rent and office bills were affordable, I was making just enough to make ends meet. Because of this, I started to consider adding other areas of focus to my practice, such as workshops, speaking, and yoga classes. After completing yoga teacher training, I knew for sure that I wanted to add yoga classes to my offerings due to the therapeutic benefits, such as reduced stress, mindfulness, improved sleep, and enhanced mental health. The office space that I was renting wasn't ideal for guiding small yoga and meditation classes. After much thought, I decided that it was time for me to venture out and find an office space in which I could practice both as a therapist and yoga guide. My hope was that this new addition would help me find joy in my business again and create additional income. I talked the plan over with my husband, and he gave me his full support. I prayed about it and felt confident in my decision to take on this new business venture. Now, don't get me wrong, this wasn't a quick decision. It took several months of contemplation before moving forward with the idea.

The first decision that I had to make was the location. Just like any business, your clients will be based on your location. I sought support from a small business development organization that I had come across during COVID, and they helped me with market research, including my client's full demographics. Having the market research gave me the courage that I needed to sit down and map out how much money I needed to move, the pros and cons of the area that I chose and if I could afford all of the additional expenses such as security systems, business Wi-Fi, renter's insurance, highway tolls, extra gas for my car due to the new distance and new furniture pieces to add to what I already had. *"Easy Peezy!"* I thought, *"I've got this, and I have support"*.

Radical Tenderness

We found the place for my new space! My husband and I were taking an afternoon ride, and we drove into the area of Houston where I wanted to open my office. While driving we turned down a street that I was familiar with. This street was quiet and filled with a mixture of homes and small businesses. There were these cute little business offices that almost looked like cottages. Each office was about 200 square feet, and all had their own entrances. It was perfect! We both noticed a sign stuck in the ground in front of the parking lot entrance that read, "space for lease." I said to my husband, *"I will only consider this space if the corner office is available"*. The cottages, if you will, were shaped kind of like the capital letter L. I wanted the corner office because I knew I would be offering sound meditation with crystal quartz bowls, and it would reduce neighbor disturbance. There was a telephone number listed on the sign. I called the number as we were looking around the area. Can you believe this? The owner of the property picked up the call and said, *"I am right around the corner. I just finished showing the office to someone, and I can come back if you'd like."* What are the chances of this happening? Of course, I said yes!

Radical Tenderness

We waited for her arrival, and she was there within 10 minutes. As she pulled up, I could see her getting the keys to the space, and it was the corner office at the entrance. I think my heart hit my stomach with disbelief. We greeted one another, and I shared information with her about my background and my business plans. We walked into the office space, and I could see my vision coming to life. It only needed a few minor things, such as paint changes and the removal of a water system that I wouldn't need. We discussed numbers and how long it would take for the space to be ready. The owner informed me that she was waiting to hear back from another interested person regarding the space, and they had a certain amount of time to reply before she would consider moving forward with me as the potential renter. After our meeting concluded, I had decided that the space was mine. The weekend went by, and I was still bubbling with excitement about all the possibilities and how this new space could help both current and future clients.

On the following Monday morning, the owner called to inform me that the space was mine. We discussed the lease agreement and the fees associated with the first month's rent. I was elated and scared all at the same time. I was able to end my previous lease with no problem, and off I went to new beginnings. I moved into the new space with ease. We packed my old office and moved into the new office all in a matter of a day. I was ready for new clients and a new way of practicing. In this new space, I could walk the neighborhood, attend my own yoga classes at the yoga studio down the street, and truly practice self-care while working in an environment that felt aligned with my brand. Besides being a great environment, my office had kind neighbors, and it felt like a community where we all looked out for each other. In addition to self-care, I was also able to have non-traditional meetings with clients, such as walking with them while talking, meetings at the closest coffee shop, and sitting on the patio area of my office. I was attracting new clients and able to hold one-to-one yoga sessions and sound healing with them. It was true joy, until it wasn't. The dream went away in a little over a year of being in the new space.

One morning, I pulled into the parking lot of my office, and all the glass was broken from my neighbor's office door. I am usually the first one to arrive at my suite due to my early start. I begin seeing clients at 7 am most mornings, which meant that I was often arriving at the office before daylight hit to prepare for my day. I saw all the glass on the ground, and I thought to myself, *"Oh my gosh, what if the person who broke into the office is still in there?"* One thing is for sure, and two things are for certain: I was not getting out of my car. I called my office neighbor, to whom the suite belonged, but she didn't answer, probably because it was around 6:30 am. Then I called the building owner and informed her of the break-in, and she asked me to call the police, which I did. The police came, and I finally got in touch with my office neighbor. Let me remind you that I have a 7 am client on the schedule. I had to cancel the client because we now have a crime scene, and my office has become the police station. This was too much action for 6:30 in the morning!

While this was all going on, I hadn't realized that my stress response had kicked up a notch. My anxiety hit a peak. I was anxious for most of the day, but I knew I had people depending on me for support, so I kept going on with my day as if nothing ever happened. I was also saying to myself, this didn't happen to "me," so I have no reason to be worried or anxious. Well, it did affect me, and the fact that I tried to convince myself to ignore the whole thing was not good. This way of behaving and thinking was normal to me though because it was how I had learned to survive chaos.

From that day forward, I drove to my office and pulled into the parking lot on guard. I could feel butterflies in my stomach and tightness in my body. The feelings often went away once I was in my office and settled in.

A couple of months passed by, and I was still ignoring my feelings. Besides, I had tolerated worse. Or at least that is what I convinced myself to believe. This was issue number one. I ignored the symptoms and body signals.

I have now signed my lease for another year, hoping that things will be better. Again, this was my dream space. I am about 3 months into the new lease. Things are going well. I have no complaints, and I am trying to put the year before behind me. I am seeing clients; business is picking up. I now feel like my original intention is manifesting. One of the ways I practice self-care while working is by drinking a bottle of water during sessions. I do this because it forces me to get up and walk to the restroom, and I also believe it's a practice to release anything I may have been holding energetically while in session. The restroom was about four office doors away from my office, which allowed me to get up, enjoy the fresh air, and experience the elements. Our community shared restroom was like our offices; it had its own door, its own AC/Heat, and its own lock. Entry into the restroom required an access code. Once inside the restroom, there was a lock, when you turn to the left, you unlock the door, and when you turn to the right, the door locks. From the outside, the lock shows red when occupied and green when vacant. The door was kind of old, and the lock would often stick.

Radical Tenderness

A couple of times, I asked myself, *"What if this lock gets stuck one day?"* I would chuckle at the idea of how funny it would be if someone got stuck in the bathroom. Can you imagine that?

I normally see between six and eight clients a day, and I walk to the restroom at least four times during my work hours. I had my restroom time down to a science. It would take me 5 minutes max, which includes using the restroom, washing my hands, and getting back to my seat in the office. This type of restroom training came from my years of working in customer service, where a 15-minute break would need to be divided for restroom use. God forbid if you had to do number two, all your break time is used up!

It was a normal day, and I was doing my normal routine: drinking my water and walking to the restroom. I was mid-way through my morning, which means I had met with at least 4 clients. I was practicing business as usual. I went to the restroom, finished my business, and washed my hands. I went to unlock the door, and the door lock on the inside was not moving. I say to myself, *"Okay, the lock gets stuck all the time, no big deal."* I take a deep breath and try the lock again. It's not moving. Guess who wasn't chuckling now, ME. I keep trying the lock, and it's not working. This can't be real life! Now I am starting to panic, my palms are sweaty, my heart is beating fast, I am getting hot, and just like that, I am in a full-blown panic attack.

I couldn't think straight. I didn't have my phone, which meant I couldn't call anyone. I thought you could use your watch, *"Shit, my watch won't work because it says that I am too far away from my phone. I am trapped! AND I have a client waiting for me for a virtual visit. "Okay, what do I do now?"* is what I am asking myself.

I started banging on the door and the walls of the bathroom, hoping and wishing that someone would hear me. The person who had an office connected to the restroom is rarely in her suite, so I knew it was unlikely she would come save me. I am now in the restroom for about 15 minutes. I tried to push the door. I tried to kick the door. In my mind, I was strong enough to break the door down. Nope, I wasn't. I kept convincing myself to relax. I knew someone would have to use the restroom sooner or later and discover that I was in there. At this point, though, I am now worried about my client. What is she thinking, because I am never this late, and I don't want her to worry about me. I also hope she doesn't think that I have abandoned her by not showing up for her today. I care about my clients, and I understand what it takes to show up for yourself at any capacity, especially in therapy.

Then I started working on a plan in case no one came to save me. My plan was to keep myself hydrated by drinking water from the faucet, and I would stay cool because the AC was manual. I may have forgotten to tell you that this situation happened during a Houston Hot summer! I could also close the lid on the toilet to have a place to sit. If I ended up staying there until the end of the workday, my husband would surely come looking for me. I know, I know this plan is irrational, but that is what my anxiety looks like. Now I know you are thinking, of course, someone is coming to "save you." It surely did not seem like anyone was coming, and I was used to feeling and behaving like NO ONE was coming to save me.

Time was ticking, and it felt like I was "stuck" in the bathroom for hours. I am still banging on the door and walls, hoping, and praying to be heard. Eventually, I heard someone attempt to use the access code to unlock the door; of course, they could not get in because the door was locked from the inside. I started hitting the door, telling them that I was stuck in the bathroom, and the inside lock would not work. She told me that she was going to get help. While she was getting help, another suite mate, Kristen, needed to use the restroom, so I repeated that I was stuck. She recognized my voice and said, *"Oh my God, Lakeisha, is that you?"* I said yes, and now the tears finally started. Her words were, *"Hang in there, we are going to get you out."* A few minutes later, I heard Daniel's voice, our other suite mate. He had some tools that he was using to try to unscrew the lock off, but that did not work. Meanwhile, Kristen is providing words of assurance that everything was going to be okay. Daniel couldn't get the lock off, so he called our landlord, and she called our maintenance person to come address the issue. We all waited for him, which seemed like another couple of forevers. He got there and began working on the lock, and it was really stuck; nothing that he did was working. I started hearing power tools at work. He had to remove part of the door frame to get the door open. He opened the door, and everyone clapped. While they were clapping, I felt like collapsing. With all this action happening, I am sweaty, tearful, and flooded with feelings of anxiety. But I was relieved. I expressed my gratitude to everyone and walked back to my office, a hot ass mess. I took one breath and called my client. She was worried. I spared her the details but told her the bathroom door had locked and had gotten stuck. I apologized for missing my appointment and rescheduled her for another day within the week. I finished my workday, saw the last few clients, and proceeded to go home as usual. This was issue number two. I ignored the effects of the traumatic bathroom event that day.

I wasn't honoring my nervous system. I was operating in survival mode. I pushed the incidents to the side and convinced myself they were no big deal because I had experienced what I considered worse things. Also, I was in therapy and talked to my therapist about what

Radical Tenderness

I had experienced. As I recall our processing of the events during those times, I can now understand why she was concerned that I wasn't concerned. I also remember her telling me that I was in survival mode and I needed to rest. Did I listen? Nope, I sure didn't. I just knew what I had been doing to manage my symptoms was enough. I was going to therapy bi-weekly, actively use coping skills, yoga, prayer, meditation, journaling, connecting with nature, spending time with my husband, and maintaining my social connections. In the past all these things worked. But my nervous system was overworked. Those two events contributed to a slippery slope of anxiety and depression. My panic attacks, that I thought were never coming back, started happening again. It was horrible.

This time, it felt like the attacks came back with a plan to snipe me out. I found myself driving to work and feeling dizzy at least 2 days a week. I would wake up to thoughts that something "bad" was going to happen. My chest stayed tight, and there was tension in my shoulders. I had silent meltdowns in the car at least 2 times a week. I normally talk to my "sister-cousin" on the way to work in the morning. During one of our morning conversations, panic hit me out of nowhere while I was driving. I started feeling dizzy, my heart was racing, and my palms were sweating, just that quickly. I told her that I was having a panic attack. Because we talked most mornings, she knew how I had been feeling. I remember hearing her say, "No one should feel like this every day." I was thankful that I could share how I was feeling with her. Sharing my feelings, my true, deep feelings, was something I rarely did. Everyone had their own version of me being "okay". At this point, I felt like I was screaming, and no one could hear me. Also, I am a therapist. Therapists are supposed to have self-awareness; they are supposed to be able to keep things under control, right? Wrong. Yes, I am a therapist. I am also very human. I am someone who has had to work through life's difficulties just like everyone else. Being a therapist does not make me immune to any mental health disorder or dis-ease. The dis-ease had consistently returned. I could no longer wait for anyone to hear me. It was time for me to listen to myself. I did what felt like the hardest thing: admitting that what I had been doing was no longer working and that I needed something more.

I talked with my therapist about medication and told her that I would be calling a psychiatrist to get more help. My therapist supported my decision, and I made the call. There was a lot of guilt and shame that came with taking medication. This was not something that I felt I needed in the past. It was also hard to admit to myself that I couldn't handle what I was experiencing on my own any longer. In addition to starting medication, I made another very difficult decision: I gave up my dream office space. I broke the lease early and found another location. For the next year, I dealt with feelings of shame, guilt, and failure. Depression hit me hard, which meant more self-care needed to happen. I had to make radical changes.

To maintain my ethical standards as a clinician, I reduced my client caseload to ensure I could take care of myself before helping others care for themselves.

I felt like a failure. I had the self-awareness, I was doing "all of the things". But was I really? Yes, and I allowed myself to fall victim to a faulty narrative. The narrative, "I couldn't fail" kept me on a hamster wheel, running the marathon of a façade. We must be honest and have real conversations with ourselves. I am not talking about the realness of "Girl Get Yourself Together". I am talking about the part of you that says, "Girl, you had a setback and it's okay, we can begin again". Healing takes time, and you can start as often as you need to. So, what if the same thing keeps coming back up? If it does, that could possibly mean it's a perpetual issue that may call for support, or maybe you never really dealt with the issue in the first place. As much as I would like to think that I had control over my anxiety, it very much had taken control over me. This time, I didn't take the route of diving deep into my childhood to look back at my shadow or wounds, if you will. I started exactly from the current source of pain. The source of my pain was in my control. I ignored my own needs because I was so concerned about being available for others, family, friends, and clients that I had forgotten about my own needs. I had forgotten that I mattered.

You must take care of yourself before even considering how to care for someone else. You are the most important person that you have in your life. I know this concept can often be difficult to digest, but self-neglect is very real, and it can lead you to the road of self-criticism, self-judgement, and poor overall health.

Always remember that you matter; you matter the most.

Pause to return to yourself.

Reconnect with your self-compassionate inner voice and gently release the residue of survival mode.

Set Your Intention:

Find a quiet, safe, and comfortable space. Sit or lie down. Consider adding instrumental music, lighting your favorite candle, or choosing a grounding object (e.g. favorite photo, affirmation card, or prayer beads).

Breathwork Practice (5-7 minutes)

1. **Arrival Breath**

    Inhale slowly through the nose for 4 counts

    Hold for 2 counts

Exhale gently through the mouth for 6 counts

Repeat, allowing your body to settle

2. **Body Scan with Breath**

    Bring awareness to your body from head to toe

    With each exhale, imagine releasing tension from a specific area (e.g., shoulders, jaw, heart space)

    Whisper to yourself: "I am safe to feel."

3. **Box Breathing**

    Inhale for 4 counts

    Hold for 4 counts

    Exhale for 4 counts

    Hold for 4 counts

    Repeat for 4–6 rounds

    Visualize a square of light surrounding you with each breath cycle

4. **Affirmation**

    Inhale: "I honor my needs."

    Exhale: "I release what no longer serves me."

5. **Closing Breath**

    Return to natural breathing

Place one hand on your heart, one on your belly

Whisper: "I am here. I matter."

Reflective Journaling:

These prompts are an invitation to reflect on survival, vulnerability, and renewal.

Name Your Experience

- What signs has your body given that you have ignored?
- In what ways have you convinced yourself that your pain is "normal"?
- What have you feared will happen if/when you need to admit that you're not okay?

Unpack Survival Mode

- How has survival mode shaped your responses to stress?
- What narratives have you internalized about strength, failure, and control?

Reclaim Self-Compassion

- What does your nervous system need to feel safe again?
- How can you honor your humanity while still holding space for others?
- What does "beginning again" mean to you in this moment?

Renewal

- What message would you write to the version of you who may have felt trapped, unseen, or overwhelmed?

Radical Tenderness

- What boundaries or practices can you implement to protect your peace?
- What does holding space for yourself look like now—not just physically, but emotionally?

Radical Tenderness

Radical Tenderness

11

The Gift of Self-Compassion: Choosing Tenderness Over Tough Love

I have often been called the "strong friend'. Being overly responsible or being one of the strong friends comes with a cost. For me, the cost was not sharing my emotions and being the worst inner critic that you can imagine. I thought holding in what was bothering me showed the world that I was strong. Growing up in a household where domestic violence occurred any given Monday through Sunday taught me how to ignore pain and "save face". Masking my pain became a normal response, even when the feelings were positive. I constantly told myself that I needed to be better, stronger, and that my feelings weren't important enough to address. After all, it felt like nobody cared to listen. While this probably wasn't true at all, my experiences told me otherwise.

My survival tactic was tough love. I didn't know how to be kind to myself. I began to internalize the external messages that I received from others such as your "too much" or "doing too much". It wasn't until I started therapy that I began to realize how critical I was of myself. I had no conscious awareness of the negative effect that my inner dialogue was having on my self-esteem and how it was contributing to my symptoms of anxiety. My internal critic was keeping me in a state of worry and made me feel hopeless.

One of the skills that my therapist taught me to address my thoughts was "thought stopping". Thought stopping is a cognitive behavioral therapy technique that can help interrupt negative thought cycles. The goal was for me to address the thoughts that were contributing to the inner criticism. While thought stopping and other approaches, such as thought challenging and fact finding, were helpful, there seemed to be some sort of mental block that kept me teetering between being able to practice the skill and seeing the manifestation of the positive outcomes of the skill.

The thought-stopping technique worked, but viewing myself in a positive light just wasn't happening. Behind the negative thoughts was the narrative of me telling myself that I wasn't enough. The narrative had to be dismantled. During one of my therapy sessions, my therapist asked me a question that empowered me to change my perspective.

She said, *"If your friend was feeling how, you are feeling or criticizing themselves the way that you are, what would you tell them?"*. Of course, I had all the answers. I explained how I would encourage them, be patient with them, and be kind towards them. She asked, *"What prevents you from being that person to yourself?"*

What caused me to pause at that moment was not knowing that I needed to be a friend to myself. Instead of leaning into my feelings, I pushed them away and acted as if they didn't exist. Instead of validating my feelings, I told myself they didn't matter. It made a recipe for self-sabotage. Being a friend to myself started with identifying parts of me that I liked, and not just the external parts. It was a call to action to search my heart and find the tender space that needed to have a softness, a tender voice. I had to give myself the gift of self-compassion, the sacred space between self-respect and self-love.

I had to offer myself the same, non-judgmental, supportive understanding, and acceptance that I so freely gave to others. I had to create an internal sanctuary that cultivated self-compassion. Once I realized how deeply I needed that gentleness, I started leaning into the practices that could help me show up for myself.

These practices helped to remind me that I am also worthy of the same care that I freely give.

Practices to Cultivate Self-Compassion:

In exploring practices to cultivate self-compassion, I invite you to pause, listen inwardly, and honor the tender spaces where growth and care begin.

Mirror Work:

Look into your own eyes and say, "I forgive myself for harsh judgment and criticism. I honor my effort to change. I forgive my missteps and welcome a friendship."

Self-Compassion Journaling:

Write a letter to yourself from the voice of someone who loves you unconditionally.

Boundary + Grace Check-In:

Ask yourself weekly: "Where did I honor my limits?" and "Where can I offer myself softness and support?"

Affirmation:

I am worthy.

I meet myself in the middle of self-respect and self-love with grace.

12

The Strong Friend: Releasing the Role and Reclaiming Your Needs

Have you ever experienced a moment when something suddenly clicked, revealing a truth you didn't even know you needed?
It was the end of a workday, and my normal routine is to put my work bag in the passenger seat, put my water bottle in the cup holder, and find something to listen to for a few minutes before making phone calls during the ride home. Calling a friend or family member to and from work was something that I did often. It was my way of connecting because most of my friends and family live on the East Coast, and I am an hour behind them in time zone. They were usually off work by the time I got off, and our drives home made it easy to connect.

Radical Tenderness

This particulate afternoon, instead of my normal routine, I found myself walking to the car carrying the weight of the day. There was a sense of heaviness in my chest. I was having a bad day, I was riddled with feelings of overwhelm, and by the time I sat down in the driver's seat, tears were just streaming down my face. I was tired. I looked at my phone to scan my contacts to see who I could call for support. Because I usually talk to the same few people a week, I went straight to my call log. Before I hit the call icon, I felt the urge to scan my incoming and outgoing calls. One of the benefits of having an iPhone is that it keeps months of your call logs. I scrolled my call log, and to my surprise, for months, I had more outgoing calls than incoming calls. That moment and call log provided clarity.

I was "the strong friend" — the one who held everyone else up. The one who checked-in, offered support, and made sure others were okay. But the truth is, I was exhausted. I didn't even realize I had stepped into that role or how I showed up until I looked at my call log. Sitting with this new revelation forced me to acknowledge all the ways I had been showing up for everyone: physically, mentally, emotionally, spiritually, and sometimes even financially. I also had to take accountability for over giving without reciprocity.

I was behaving selflessly. The more selfless I became, the less of myself I had left. Eventually, I was empty — and if I'm honest, I think I started empty. My giving and my strength weren't signs that I had it all together, nor were they rooted in my profession. Deep down, the "strong friend" was the person I needed for myself.

For years, I tried to be the person for others that I desperately needed someone to be for me. But something had to change. I had to change. I had to unlearn avoidance, pretending I was fine, minimizing my emotions, and overextending my time and resources. I kept hoping that if I gave enough, I would eventually receive the same in return. Instead, that hope turned into resentment and a growing disconnection from myself and the people around me.

On that day in the car, I felt weak — worn down by years of carrying the weight of others' pain while ignoring my own. Yes, I had been to therapy and was still attending, but a part of me believed that at some point I was going for the sake of others, not myself. That moment became a turning point. I decided it was time to consider *me* and what I needed.

I began by asking myself each day, "Lakeisha, how are you doing? How are you feeling?" It took months before I could answer honestly. From there, I shifted into setting intentions and taking small, meaningful actions to meet my own needs. It started with simple steps: drinking water first thing in the morning, scheduling time to feel my emotions, allowing myself to cry when I needed to, and moving my body to release what I had been holding.

Have you ever found yourself identifying as the "strong friend"?

If you saw yourself in these words, don't rush past that.

This is your cue to pause.

To check in.

To ask yourself the questions you've been too busy, too tired, or too strong to ask.

Start here. Start now.

Pause to Release the Role of Being a Strong Friend.

Release the role that you've taken on to connect with who you are, who you want to be and how you want to show up for yourself.

Set Your Intention:

Release the weight of being "the strong one" and reconnect with your needs.

Breathwork Practice (5-7 minutes):

1. **Settle In**

   Close your eyes or soften your gaze.

   Let your shoulders drop.

   Place one hand on your heart space, the other on your belly.

   Take a moment to ask yourself gently:

   "How am I feeling right now?"

   No need to fix—just notice.

2. **Breath**

   This pattern helps calm the nervous system and create space for emotional release.

   Inhale through your nose for a count of **4**

   (Feel your belly rise beneath your hand)

   Hold the breath for a count of **6**

   (Let the stillness hold you—not your strength)

   Exhale slowly through your mouth for a count of **8**

   (Imagine releasing the weight you've been carrying)

3. **Gentle Affirmation**

   After your final exhale, place both hands over your heart and whisper to yourself:

Radical Tenderness

"I am allowed to need. I am allowed to rest. I am allowed to be held."

Stay here for a few more breaths. Let your body know it's safe to soften.

Reflective Journaling:

To the friend who always shows up for others:

Check in with yourself.

- What does "strong" look like in your life right now—and is it serving you?
- When was the last time you asked yourself, "How am I really doing?"
- What emotions have you been carrying quietly, and where do you feel them in your body?

Unpack the Role

- In what ways have you been showing up for others more than you've shown up for yourself?
- What parts of the "strong friend" role feel true to who you are, and what parts feel learned or expected?
- What do you need to unlearn about strength, vulnerability, and worthiness?

Radical Tenderness

Reclaim Space

- What does support look like when it's reciprocal?
- What boundaries do you need to set to protect your emotional energy?
- How can you create space to feel without rushing to fix or explain?

Return to Self

- What small, daily acts help you reconnect with yourself?
- How do you want to feel at the end of the day—and what helps you get to that feeling?
- What would it look like to be the friend you've always needed, to yourself?

Radical Tenderness

Radical Tenderness

13

Faith Unbound: Losing Religion to Find Divine Love

I come from a large family of gospel singers. We are the type of family in which you can expect a rendition of gospel singing and prayer at the family gatherings. The town in Maryland that I am from is small, but my family is well-known for their singing. My grandmother and her siblings travel around the state to sing at funerals, weddings, or church services. They are constantly called upon. My grandmother has the type of Soprano tone and bravado that will bring you to your knees in a state of surrender whenever she sings, no matter what your faith or religious belief is. She is specifically known for singing, the gospel song "Order My Steps". I can hear her singing as I am writing and feel the chill in my heart; her voice is just that powerful. The gift of song was passed down to several family members, and now the younger generation has joined the elders to help keep the tradition alive.

Growing up going to church was somewhat of a requirement. My Grandmother is the type of grandmother that ensured all her grandchildren went to church most Sundays. She made sure that we were at church looking presentable, which included having on a slip under our dresses and wearing opaque tights in the colder months and pantyhose in the warmer months. She also made sure that we showed up for church activities. One of my grandmother's sisters was the orchestrator for all the activities that the youth were involved in, which included Sunday school, vacation Bible study, Christmas caroling, and any church activity for children that you could think of. Her sister loved children; you could feel it. She would round up all her great nieces and nephews and pour her heart and soul into us.

We all had responsibilities at church, which included reading scripture during service, collecting offering, participating in holiday plays and becoming an acolyte. Being an acolyte was one of my responsibilities. An acolyte prepares the altar for Sunday services. As hymns were being sung at the beginning of services, I would be dressed in my white robe, carrying a beautiful brass candle lighter which was used to light the candles that were placed on the altar, one on each side of the cross. Although I didn't completely understand the meaning of the ritual, I felt proud and could sense the sacredness that lighting the candles ushered into the space of the church. I still carry this practice with me today with my home altar. Religion was always the center of my upbringing by way of the elders in our family.

There were many things about the church that I didn't understand. As I got older and into my teenage years, all the way into my adulthood, I began to pull away from church for many reasons, one of the prominent reasons was feeling like I didn't belong. I could sing the song "Yes, Jesus Loves Me." I could quote scripture and even recite "The Apostles Creed," which is a tradition during United Methodist Church service; however, as I grew older, I realized I did not believe that Jesus loved me. What I was told to believe and what I was told to do, such as pray, got lost in the midst of the suffering that I witnessed in my home. Many nights out of the week, I could expect to witness the domestic violence that my mother endured from her partner at the time, who was also my father, in addition to the other two partners that she had after him. I often stepped into the role of being her protector. I endured physical and emotional assaults in the crossfire of violence. I began to lose hope and religion. I made a vow to myself that when I turned 18, I would move as far away as possible so that I would never have to go through what I went through again. My search for hope and safety led me down many paths as a teen and young adult that exacerbated the trauma that I had experienced in my home. God, and I became very distant friends.

Finding Faith.

I was reintroduced to Christianity by way of a friend from middle school, whom I had reconnected with once I had "moved far away". She shared with me all of the ways that God had changed her life and how her church family supported and loved her. We both experienced a similar upbringing; therefore, my thought was, if becoming a Christian worked for her, surely it would work for me. I decided to give Christianity a full try. I started watching church services on television, listening to several types of Christian music, purchased my first Bible, and started my new way of living. The exploration of my newfound faith was not as easy as I've written. I now had to find and connect with a new community. So, I did. I became a "church girl". I did all the things that I thought would make me a "good person". I paid tithes and offerings, I participated in Bible studies, services, and joined different ministries that I thought I would be good at. I thought becoming a Christian would equate to being loved, feeling safe, and feeling accepted. I progressed in knowing scripture, serving, leading, and being a "perfect believer." I began placing my church family in categories that were parallel to family roles. I thought because I had chosen this family and the faith, it would be pure bliss. But that was not what I experienced. I experienced happiness, I did experience love, and a sense of family; however, I also experienced judgment and criticism. The judgment and criticism often weighed heavily on my mind and in my heart eventually I felt out of place, distant, and broken hearted.

I believe one of the reasons the judgment and criticism weighed so heavily on my mind was because it was something I had grown accustomed to in my upbringing. But I didn't think that I would experience some of the same things in the church. I have come to understand and accept that Church members are human. They are not perfect; I am not perfect. Unfortunately, there were many situations that I experienced as a church member that triggered me and reminded me of some of the traumatic things that I had experienced in my nuclear family. I was literally going to church for years with a heavy heart and leaving the same way that I came. The happiness and breakthroughs at the altar had fleeting moments, and I often found myself feeling depressed because I wasn't changing. I did all the actions of being a Christian, and I couldn't understand why I was still feeling the same after leaving church. At some point, the pain in my heart became so heavy that I separated myself from church again. Success was showing on the outside, but on the inside, I felt horrible. Looking back on the experience, I genuinely believe that the experience worked out for my highest good. The separation gave me an opportunity to really seek out God in many ways that I wasn't accustomed to. I also had to unlearn rules and religious teachings that no longer aligned with who God created me to be.

"I am not a Christian", is what I said while walking and talking to a friend on the phone one morning. If you just felt a jolt in your heart, that's exactly what I felt as the words came out of my mouth. I said out loud what I had been feeling for so long. Because I knew to fear God, I started to feel like something bad was about to happen to me because of what I said out loud. Out of fear, I started praying and hoping that I wasn't going to be doomed to Hell. I sat with my statement for a couple of days and grieved the idea that I no longer identified with a religion that I had been taught since my formative years. I thought about my grandmother and how she would feel if she had heard me say those words. I thought about other Christians who are near and dear to my heart and began to worry about what they would think of me. I had to let go of all that worry because the statement that I made was really about me, my experiences, and God. It had everything to do with our relationship and nothing to do with my relationship with others.

On that day, what really happened was a surrender, a letting go of what was so that I could truly receive who God is to me and for me. I had been hiding in my religion, hoping to feel what I had heard people talk about when they described God. I couldn't feel or experience what people were describing because I was looking externally, and I needed to go inward. Finding my faith has been one of the hardest things that I've ever had to do and continue to work on daily. Along the journey, I gave myself permission to explore. My intention was and is to see God everywhere, in everything, and in everyone, always. In the seeking, I began to discover that what I was looking for all along was within me; the love that I was looking for was already in me. I needed God to help me to cultivate it. I lost my religion to gain my faith by returning to God's love without judgment, without criticism, without fear, just wholehearted love. A sacred relationship between God and I developed that no one needed to convince me of.

And if after reading my words, you are wondering where I stand on my faith, I absolutely love God, I love and believe in Jesus Christ. Faith is my compass. My faith guides and replenishes me daily.

Before you move forward, I invite you to take a moment to return to yourself and settle into what is true for you.

Breath, release, and reconnect to your compass.

Pause to connect to what guides and grounds you.

Reconnect with your inner sanctuary and release any inherited fear, judgment, or shame.

Set your Intention:

Find a quiet space. Sit or lie down. Allow yourself to be present.

Breathwork Practice (5-7 minutes):

1. **Inhale deeply** through the nose for 4 counts, imagining the breath as light entering your heart space.

2. **Hold for 4 counts**, visualizing the light warming your heart.

3. **Exhale slowly** through your mouth for 6 counts, releasing any fear or judgment you've internalized.

4. **Repeat for 5–7 cycles**, whispering inwardly:

    "I am safe. I am sacred. I am held."

5. **Close** your eyes and place your hands over heart, honoring your faith, religion, or spiritual lineage and your present truth.

Reflective Journaling:

I invite you to reflect on your spiritual identity, and the reclamation of divine love.

Sacred Redefinition:

- What does faith mean to you? How does it show up in your daily life?

Healing the Inner Child:

- What would you say to the younger version of yourself who felt unloved or unsafe in spiritual spaces?

Spiritual Autonomy:

- What practices (prayer, meditation, church services) or beliefs feel most authentic to your relationship with God today?

Reconciliation & Release:

- What fears or judgments are you ready to release in to deepen your spiritual connection?

14

The Arrival: Coming Home to My Body, Reconnecting Through Breath, Movement, and Presence

What is this chanting all about? Those were my thoughts as I lay on the yoga studio floor in supine position, flat on my back, and torso facing upward. I wasn't comfortable with being still for what seemed like an hour, but it was really three to five minutes. This stillness created a discomfort that I have never experienced before. My mind seemed to be all over the place. It also didn't help that I was in this foreign place —a yoga studio —with people who didn't look like me, and I didn't understand a word they were saying. The class was small and intimate; incense burned, with a scent of patchouli or something close to it. The lights were dimly lit, and everyone seemed very calm.

Radical Tenderness

I had never witnessed anything like this before. Everyone had their own mat and were sitting on the floor in full lotus pose. The room was noticeably quiet and still.

The class started, and it seemed the people in the room were experts because every time the teacher spoke, they knew exactly what to do. The teacher was speaking Sanskrit and teaching by way of hand gestures. The teacher was not actually getting into the poses, but everyone was following the spoken cues. Oddly enough, I was beginning to flow with the class. Somehow, I made it through the class. To this day, being able to flow through an hour-long yoga class taught in Sanskrit, which was a language that I did not understand at the time, still baffles me. I was invited to the yoga class by a friend who thought that it would be a great idea to try something new.

I have always had an adventurous way about myself; of course, I was willing to try the class. I was also at the beginning of my personal counseling journey, and I had read and heard about this "yoga" that was supposed to help calm the mind. Before class, I envisioned myself twisted like a pretzel, wondering how that was going to be possible. Also, I had never seen or heard of a black person going to yoga, which meant that I had to show up in the room with people of other races, predominantly Caucasian, who appeared to be thin, eat healthy, very happy, and carefree. Meanwhile, my internal world was crumbling. Why not give yoga a try? Worst-case scenario, I would leave the same way that I came. In the best-case scenario, I would experience some of the happiness I saw, and maybe it would help me become "happy". During the whole class, my friend and I would occasionally glance at each other with the look of "What the Hell did we sign up for?".

Once class ended, we got in her car and laughed at each other during the car ride home. We never returned to that yoga class; however, there was something about the class that kept coming back to my memory. It was that feeling that I had at the end of class, which was the inability to be still. Why couldn't I relax? Maybe it was because I was in an environment that was foreign to me, or maybe it was because of the stories that I had heard about yoga being an idol-worshipping practice. I couldn't quite identify clearly what it was, but what felt "louder" wasn't the environment or the stories that I had heard. It was my inability to experience a sense of ease and calmness in my mind and body. I had been in survival mode for so long that my nervous system was dysregulated.

Fast forward 15 years: after moving to a new state, getting a new job, and making new friends, a co-worker and I started a weight-loss journey, and she told me about a Bikram Yoga class she wanted to try that was around the corner from her house. She had heard that

Bikram Yoga could help with weight loss due to the room being so heated. Now you notice I said heated. Again, I am curious, so I decided to attend class with her. What she did not tell me was that the class was 90 minutes, 26 postures, and that the room temperature was 105 degrees with 40% humidity.

The setting up of this class was a little different than my first yoga experience. It was slightly bigger, about 20 people in the room, and the walls were full-length mirrors except for the entrance wall and the back wall. There were ballet bars around the room, which I soon learned were for support if needed for several postures during the class. Before class began, the instructor said, "Focus on staying in the room". Five minutes into the class I understood exactly why she gave that instruction. It felt like the heat turned up a notch; it really didn't, it was just my mind focusing on the heat. She also said, "You can take a knee or lie down at any point during the class". She was offering an invitation to honor both my feelings and my body. I followed her instructions and successfully completed my first Bikram Yoga class.

That night I slept like a baby. I hadn't slept that well in years due to having night terrors and being on high alert. Because of that sweet sleep and feeling of ease in my body, I decided to sign up for the 10 class in 30 days challenge. Don't get me wrong, there was some reservation because I said to myself when signing up, "Why am I doing this?"

The more classes I attended, the more connected to my body I felt. I could hear myself breathe. I could feel areas of tension that I hadn't noticed before. I had the opportunity to internally inquire about the tension and discover if it was connected to a feeling in my body or a thought in my mind. At times, it was both. In addition to the "noticing," I was looking at myself directly in the mirror as my body made shapes in response to the instructor's guidance. I had never witnessed myself in such a nonjudgmental, non-critical, soft way before. I can even remember times when I spoke softly, encouraging myself to keep going. The more I attended, the more flexible I became, mind, body, and spirit. It felt like I was coming into alignment. I was completely present, not focused on the past or the future; I was present. I allowed the "alignment" to continue to develop.

One day in class, midway through, it felt like something internally broke. Tears came flooding down my face that were not provoked by thought or memory. Instead of wiping them, I invited them. I was able to hold everything that was happening at that moment. I had never felt so connected to myself. It was like an arrival. Much like the feeling of relief that comes after traveling on a long journey and finally coming home to sleep in your own bed. That day, in that yoga class, I arrived. Finally, I was "home" in my body after years of disconnection, and I didn't long to be anywhere else. I felt the comfort of just being.

As you take in this story, allow yourself to recognize the places where you, too, have begun to come home. Maybe it's been a quiet shift, something subtle that you can't fully name yet. Maybe it's a moment when your body softened without asking permission, or a truth rose up that you finally felt ready to hold. Whatever it looks like, honor it. These are the small openings that let you return to yourself, piece by piece, breath by breath.

Pause for your arrival.

If you have gotten to this point in the book. I would like to say thank you for being tender with yourself and doing the work in whatever way that felt was authentic to your healing journey. The journey back to you.

Set your Intention:

Find a quiet space. Sit or lie down comfortably. Let your body be supported.

Place one hand on your heart, the other on your belly. Close your eyes or soften your gaze.

Breathwork Practice (5-7 minutes):

1. Grounding Breath

    Inhale slowly through your nose for a count of **4**

    (Feel the breath fill your belly, ribs, then heart space)

    Exhale gently through your mouth for a count of **6**

    (Let the breath leave from heart space, ribs, then belly)

    Repeat this cycle for **5–7 cycles**, allowing your body to soften with each exhale.

    After your final cycle of breathwork whisper to yourself:

    "I am safe to be here; I am allowed to arrive at home in my body."

    Stay for a few more moments. Let your mind, body, and spirit welcome the homecoming.

Reflective Journaling:

I invite you to reflect on what "arrival" means to you. Let the journal prompts serve as a guide whenever needed to call you back to your breath, your truth, your center.

- What environments have felt unfamiliar or unsafe, and how did you respond?
- What sensations do you notice in your body when you feel safe?
- How do you know when you're present—and what helps you stay there?
- What parts of you are asking to be witnessed, held, or softened?
- How can you honor your nervous system's need for rest and regulation?
- What practices help you move from survival to ease?
- What does "coming home to yourself" look and feel like?
- How can you move through your healing journey with more tenderness and grace?

Affirmation:

I am worthy of tenderness.

Radical Tenderness

Radical Tenderness

Epilogue

To Those Healing,
I want to remind you that, You Are the Light.
If you've made it to this page, I want to say thank you. Not just for reading, but for staying with yourself. For choosing to pause, to reflect, to breathe. For choosing to heal—even when it's hard, even when it's quiet, even when no one else sees the work you're doing.
This journey isn't about perfection. It's about presence. It's about learning to sit with your story and say, "I'm still here. I'm still becoming."

You've heard pieces of my story, some tender, some tangled, some triumphant. And maybe, just maybe, you've seen glimpses of your own. That's the beauty of healing: it's personal but never isolated. We heal in community, in reflection, in the sacred act of naming what we've carried and choosing what we'll release.

If you've whispered your pain, I hope this book reminded you that your voice matters.

If you've felt unseen, I hope these pages helped you feel held.

Radical Tenderness

If you've been surviving for too long, I hope you now feel safe enough to rest.

You are worthy of support. You are worthy of softness. You are worthy of joy.

And you are not alone.

As you continue your journey, I invite you to carry this truth:
You are the light. Not just because you've endured, but because you've chosen to shine.

Keep choosing yourself. Keep speaking up. Keep becoming.

With tender loving kindness,
Lakeisha

About The Author

Dr. Lakeisha Gatling is a licensed clinical social worker, inspirational speaker, and visionary healer with over 15 years of experience in the mental health field. She is the founder of LDGatling Counseling & Consulting, PLLC, a Houston-based psychotherapy practice providing mental wellness counseling, psychoeducation, and consulting services tailored for clinicians seeking clarity and soulful alignment in their work.

Also, the creator and founder of The Nourish Haven, LLC., Dr. Gatling offers restorative retreats, workshops, and holistic experiences that integrate yoga, meditation, and spiritual self-care. Her approach to wellness blends clinical insight with embodied practices, honoring the interconnectedness of mind, body, and spirit. Dr. Gatling cultivates a non-judgmental, person-centered environment where clients discover tools for emotional attunement and resilience. Through intentional guidance, she supports outcomes such as stress reduction, anxiety and depression relief, and burnout recovery—while encouraging work-life balance and mindfulness.

With a Ph.D. in Psychology & Christian Counseling, Dr. Gatling brings a deeply integrative perspective to her work in coaching, corporate wellness, teaching, and consulting. Her practice is grounded in authenticity, emotional clarity, and holistic transformation.

Resources

Crisis Support (Immediate Help)

988 Suicide & Crisis Lifeline: Call or text 988 anytime for free, confidential support from trained crisis counselors.

Emergency Services: Dial 911 if you or someone else is in immediate danger.

Finding Support

NAMI (National Alliance on Mental Illness): Offers support, education, and advocacy, with specific resources for teens (OK2Talk) and families.

National Domestic Violence Hotline: 1-800-799-7233

SAMHSA Treatment Locator: FindTreatment.gov helps you find mental health and substance use treatment facilities.

Therapy For Black Girls: Therapy for Black Girls is an online space dedicated to encouraging the mental wellness of Black women and girls.

The Loveland Foundation: The Loveland Foundation covers the cost of therapy for Black women and invests in the professional development of BIPOC therapists.

Recommended Reading

After the Rain: Gentle Reminders for Healing, Courage and Self-Love by Alex Elle

Communication Skills for Healthier Boundaries: Express Your Needs Without Giving in or Blowing Up by Dr. LaToya Gilmore

Drama Free: A Guide to Managing Unhealthy Relationships by Nedra Glover Tawaab

Radical Compassion: Learning to Love Yourself and Your World with the Practice of RAIN by Tara Brach

Self-Compassion: The Proven Power of Being Kind to Yourself by Kristin Neff

Set Boundaries, Find Peace: A Guide to Reclaiming Yourself by Nedra Glover Tawwab

S.H.I.F.T. Keeping your Focus to Maximize your Potential by Clarindria Addison

Made in the USA
Coppell, TX
01 February 2026